FREDERICK LEONG, PH.D.
THE OHIO STATE UNIVERSITY
DEPARTMENT OF PSYCHOLOGY
142 TOWNSHEND HALL
1885 NEIL AVENUE MALL
COLUMBUS OHIO 43210-1222

Asian Americans

Achievement Beyond IQ

Asian Americans

Achievement Beyond IQ

James R. Flynn

University of Otago

LEA
LAWRENCE ERLBAUM ASSOCIATES, PUBLISHERS
1991   Hillsdale, New Jersey   Hove and London

Lawrence Erlbaum Associates, Inc., Publishers
365 Broadway
Hillsdale, New Jersey 07642

ISBN 0-8058-1110-9
LC Card No. 91-28166

Printed in the United States of America
1 2 3 4 5 6 7 8 9 10

To the memory of
Philip Ewart Vernon

"... from standing on the shoulders of giants"

Contents

Acknowledgments

The author's greatest debt is to Philip E. Vernon, that Columbus who explored the IQ and achievements of Chinese and Japanese Americans with so much intelligence and thoroughness. Vernon had only one limitation. He could not know what would only be known in the future: that these groups had inflated IQ scores because of obsolete norms.

Those who deserve thanks divide into the heroic and the very helpful. The first category includes Robert Gardner of the East-West Center who met literally dozens of requests for data; Stephen Goodell who unlocked the resources of the Library of Congress; Arthur Jensen who was persistently cooperative in the best traditions of scholarship; Thomas Sowell who not only supplied raw data but also, through his published works, influenced my overall approach to explaining group achievement. The second includes many. Richard Lynn criticized the entire manuscript and Robert Gordon raised objections to a paper summarizing its contents. Nicholas Mackintosh made several valuable comments. George Mayeske, William W. Cooley, Ronald Flaughter, Arthur A. Dole, Lawrence H. Stewart, and John Raven supplied data about various IQ studies. Christopher Jencks provided instruction about the relationship between IQ and income. Michael Levin of the US Census Bureau and Alex von Cube of the Population Reference Bureau supplied demographic data. As usual, the staff of the Educational Testing Service was both helpful and generous, Eleanor V. Horne, Barbara Hillhouse, Donald A. Rock, Paula Knepper.

Finally, all elegance of format is due to my colleague Ramesh Thakur, the fidelity of the text to Betty Larkins and Jeanette Bonar.

James R. Flynn
January 1, 1991

1

The Ice Ages
and the Sino-Japanese Brain

This book shows that Asian Americans, particularly Chinese and Japanese Americans, achieve far beyond what their mean IQ would lead us to expect.

For example, the post-war generation of Chinese Americans, those born from 1945 to 1949, had a mean IQ of 98.5 with Whites set at 100. But their achievements in terms of education, occupation, and income suggest an estimated IQ about 21 points higher than their actual IQ. This huge IQ/achievement gap partitions into a threshold factor and a capitalization factor. Chinese Americans have a lower IQ threshold for entry into higher education and high-status occupations, that is, they can gain entry with a minimum IQ 7 points lower than White Americans. Chinese Americans capitalize more effectively on their available pool of talent: 78% above the Chinese minimum actually enter high-status occupations, as opposed to only 60% of Whites, which accounts for the remaining 14 points of their IQ/achievement gap. Japanese Americans overachieve in terms of their mean IQ by about 10 points, with 3 points due to lower IQ thresholds and 7 points due to a higher capitalization rate than Whites. The preliminary data on Filipino Americans suggest a mean IQ well below Whites but achievements that have begun to approach those of Whites.

Our primary objective is to provide evidence that Asian Americans achieve far beyond the bounds of IQ. But the fact that Chinese and

Japanese Americans have mean IQs below Whites, or no higher than Whites, creates a secondary objective. It casts doubt on theories that the Sino-Japanese peoples possess some sort of genetic superiority for IQ, or perhaps intelligence, or perhaps both. This brief introduction will take on substance as we proceed and is merely meant to arouse interest. This may have been unnecessary. There are probably as many reasons for interest in Asian Americans as there are people interested in any social problem at all. My interest came from three sources: the spectacular achievements of Asians who emigrated to the United States and became Asian Americans; skepticism about theories which claim that the mean IQs of American ethnic groups determine their fate; skepticism about evolutionary theories which claim that Chinese and Japanese are genetically superior for intelligence.

LYNN AND EVOLUTION

Richard Lynn (1987b) has produced the most detailed theory concerning the evolution of Sino-Japanese intelligence. My account of Lynn's theory attempts to solve a problem we will encounter more than once, namely, finding substitutes for terms once purely descriptive now regarded as pejorative. For example, wherever Lynn used "Mongoloid" I have substituted "Sino-Japanese". My apologies to Lynn but I believe both his work and mine will get a better reading as a result.

Lynn focused on those peoples whose original habitat was Northeast Asia, north of the Himalayas and east of the Urals, essentially the Chinese and Japanese. His theory unfolds in four steps. First, he argued that when compared to Whites, Chinese and Japanese have higher general intelligence, something he identified with the general intelligence factor measured by global IQ tests, plus a peculiar combination of higher nonverbal IQ and lower verbal IQ. Second, he argued that the IQ differences between Sino-Japanese and other races cannot be explained environmentally but should be regarded as substantially genetically programmed. Third, he proposed that the ice ages provide an evolutionary explanation of the genetic differences that set the Chinese and Japanese apart, both physically and mentally. Fourth, he provided a model for the Sino-Japanese brain which posits that the cortex devoted to nonverbal abilities has expanded at the expense of the cortex devoted to verbal abilities.

Rise and Fall of Japanese IQ

The controversy over whether Japanese have higher IQs than Whites began 13 years ago. Lynn (1977) argued that when scored against Americans with IQ set at 100, Japan had a mean IQ of 106.6, believed to be the highest IQ ever recorded for a national population. A few years later, Lynn (1982) scored the sample used to standardize the Japanese Wechsler Intelligence Scale for Children - Revised (WISC-R) against the American sample and moved his estimate upward: Japan's mean IQ now stood at 111. Since that time reanalysis plus new data has reduced that estimate by some 5 to 10 points.

Flynn (1983) argued that the scores of the Japanese WISC-R sample had been inflated by a number of factors. Lynn had used only five performance subtests in his comparison and including results from two verbal subtests cost one point. Lynn was supposedly comparing Japanese with Whites and yet the American WISC-R sample included both Whites and other races. Scoring the Japanese against only the White members of the WISC-R sample cost another two points. Finally, White Americans had gained about one point between 1972, when they were tested, and 1975, when the Japanese were tested, so that had to be deducted as well. Lynn accepted these deductions which totalled 4.4 IQ points. He then did something of great significance, that is, he expanded his comparison of Japanese with White Americans to cover fully 11 Wechsler subtests, five verbal and six performance (Lynn & Hampson, 1986). Later one performance subtest (Coding) had to be dropped because it was discovered that Japanese children had been given less time for their responses. The inclusion of a full range of verbal subtests showed that Japanese were actually below White Americans for verbal IQ and, since full scale IQ combines the verbal and performance scores, their overall WISC-R IQ now fell to 103.4. It should be noted that verbal and performance (or nonverbal) tests are quite different. The former test for things like general information, verbal comprehension, word similarities, vocabulary, and arithmetic. The latter for the ability to create a story out of pictures, see what is missing in an incomplete picture, build a design out of blocks, solve jigsaw puzzles, and code numbers.

Table 1.1 shows how the Japanese WISC-R standardization sample of 1975, children aged from 6 to 16 years, did when scored against American norms with the American mean IQ set at 100. It is based on 10 subtests and spells out the appropriate adjustments that must be made to get a fair comparison, both those that are agreed upon and those in dispute. The values

TABLE 1.1
Japanese WISC-R Standardization Sample: IQs when scored against American norms

	I	II	III	IV	V
Performance	114.6	112.0	111.0	108.8	106.8
Verbal	99.2	97.6	96.8	94.6	92.6
Full Scale	106.2	104.3	103.4	101.2	99.2

Key to scoring Japanese sample against various American norms:

I.   All Americans, 1972; Japanese sample unaltered.
II.   White Americans, 1972; Japanese sample unaltered.
III. White Americans, 1975; Japanese sample unaltered.
IV.   White Americans, 1975; allowance for urban bias.
V.   White Americans, 1975; allowance for both urban and SES bias.

Source: Lynn & Hampson, 1986, Table 3—values adjusted as described in text.

agreed upon are those labelled III which give these Japanese children a performance IQ of 111, a verbal IQ of 97, and a full scale IQ just over 103. These are not disputed because they simply score Japanese against White Americans, rather than Americans of all races, and because they assume both groups were tested in 1975, rather than at different times. The values labelled IV and V are disputed because they pose questions about whether the Japanese sample was representative and these questions cannot be answered definitively. The Japanese sample may have been affected by an urban bias, too few rural and small town children, and an elite bias in terms of socio-economic status (SES). The sample was not stratified for SES and no effort was made to ensure that the children came from homes with a typical range of parental occupations. I believe that the above estimates for Japanese IQ should be lowered by about two points, but as we shall see, the question of whether Japanese in Japan have an overall IQ of 101 or 103 or even 105 is not really important, once you see what happens to their IQ when they are reared in America.

Lynn (1987a) responded by warning that the WISC-R comparison of Japanese and Americans is only one of four reliable studies, the others involving the Columbia Mental Maturity Scale, the Differential Aptitude Test, and the New Kyoto NX. He granted that these other samples could be biased but considered this improbable and therefore, suggested taking the average of the four results, which would put Japanese IQ at 105. I would like to see these other Japanese samples put to the same searching scrutiny as the WISC-R sample, but until that is done, I concede that Japan's overall IQ could be anywhere between 101 and 105. On another matter, there is no dispute: compared to White Americans, Japanese in Japan do strikingly better on nonverbal tests, particularly those emphasizing visuospatial abilities such as visualizing shapes rotated in space, than on verbal tests. Indeed, the nonverbal versus verbal difference may amount to as much as 14 IQ points!

China and the Overseas Chinese

Turning to the Chinese, Lynn used to cite Chan (1976) as evidence that Hong Kong Chinese had a mean IQ of 113 against current British norms. However, Lynn, Hampson, and Lee (1988) have since done their own study and endorsed a figure of 104.5. Lynn (1987b) put the Chinese of Taiwan at 102 and those in Singapore at 103. Recently, Raven and Court (1989, p. 8) gave us results for mainland China itself. A sample of urban Chinese scored about 100 against British norms, after adjustment for the fact that the British subjects had been tested 7.5 years before. This range of results, 100 to 104.5, virtually duplicates the permissible range of estimates for Japanese IQ.

Genes and the Environment

Lynn (1987b) made several points against putative environmental explanations of the IQ differences between Sino-Japanese and Whites. He asserted that the most plausible variables environmentalists have to work with are socioeconomic status and family environment. As for SES, Japan, China, and the overseas Chinese of the Far East have all had per capita incomes far below America and Britain throughout most of the present century. As for family environment, he cited Stevenson, Azuma, and Hakuta (1986) to show that there is no evidence that Japanese mothers are superior to American mothers in terms of cognitive socialization techniques. Moreover, scores broken down by age show that Japanese children make IQ gains as they mature and he considered it hardly credible that Japanese parents are bad cognitive socializers of young children but good socializers of older children. Finally, Lynn believed the huge gap between Japanese nonverbal and verbal IQ poses a particularly difficult problem for environmentalists. In 1987, he noted that leading environmental theorists (including Flynn) had made no attempt to explain how environmental factors could differentiate Japanese for nonverbal and verbal abilities, and drew the inference that they simply had nothing to offer.

Having revealed the weaknesses of environmental explanations, Lynn proposed a genetic one. He emphasized that such an explanation requires an evolutionary scenario, one which shows how natural selection operating over a long period of time could have caused the appropriate genetic differences between Sino-Japanese and Whites.

The Ice Ages and the Sino-Japanese Brain

Lynn's evolutionary scenario runs as follows. Originally the human species was adapted to survival in Africa. About 120,000 years ago, some groups moved northwards into Europe and Asia and developed the pale skins which enabled them to absorb vitamin D from sunlight. For some time, these groups remained a single race but about 60,000 years ago, the ice ages began and exercised a differential effect. The population of Northeast Asia found themselves trapped by the encroaching ice from the Himalayas in the south and the Arctic in the north and were subjected to cold far more severe than the European population. In response to this extreme cold, these Asians evolved into a separate race with certain physical adaptations: an epicanthic fold and slit eyes to give protection against cold and the glare of sunlight on snow; a flattened face and shortened limbs to reduce heat loss.

The unusually hostile environment selected for general intelligence. Those who survived were those who could build well insulated shelters, make warm clothes, store food, and plan ahead to survive the severe winters. In addition, the environment selected for certain abilities at the expense of others. The human populations of that time obtained food partly by hunting and partly by gathering but the proportions differed in different latitudes. In tropical regions, plant foods were available throughout the year, so gathering was sufficient and hunting hardly necessary. In the coldest regions, the emerging Sino-Japanese racial group had to live largely by hunting and fishing because plant foods were unavailable for most of the year. Hunting effectively in Arctic conditions requires a wide range of visuospatial abilities: planning group hunting strategies, developing a good spatial map of an extensive terrain, recall of visual landmarks, perceiving prey well camouflaged against a featureless background, accurate stone throwing.

When the Sino-Japanese population became highly selected for visuospatial abilities, the most straightforward adaptation would have been a further increase in the size of the human brain. However, this would have required either larger headed babies or less mature babies whose heads grew more after birth than before. The former was forestalled by the size of the female pelvis early in human evolution and as for the latter, some constraint not understood ended the trend to less mature offspring some 250,000 years ago. Therefore, the Sino-Japanese brain could gain extra cortex for visuospatial abilities only by annexing cortex previously devoted to other abilities. For human beings in general, visuospatial abilities dominate the right cerebral hemisphere, verbal abilities the left. In Sino-Japanese, the visuospatial abilities have established a supplementary center in the left hemisphere with verbal abilities slightly reduced by the encroachment. Natural selection working on genes led essentially to a different lateralization of the brain. The trend toward visuospatial gains at the expense of verbal losses may be enhanced by environmental factors. For example, the Japanese language is rich in vowel sounds and vowel sounds seem to be processed in the right hemisphere for Whites, in the left hemisphere for Japanese. This extra task may overload the Japanese left hemisphere and lessen the efficiency of its verbal processes.

As this summary of Lynn's evolutionary theory makes clear, it puts Chinese and Japanese above Whites and Whites above Blacks for general intelligence. The theory has been amplified by Philippe Rushton and its intelligence hierarchy extended to 50 other human traits including brain size, maturation rate, sexuality, temperament, and social organization. During the recent controversy over Rushton's work, its influence was acknowledged by psychologists such as Cattell, Eysenck, Jensen, and Osborne, evolutionary biologists such as Ankney and Scott, the geneticist Gold, the sociologist Gordon, and the sociobiologist E. O. Wilson (Rushton, 1990). Their comments ranged from labeling it a promising hypothesis to opining that the weight of evidence is on its side. Naturally, they had various reservations, for example, Gold suspected that the time-span of the evolutionary scenario was too short. Snyderman and Rothman (1988) have presented survey data which show that an absolute majority of a sample of 566 American testing experts endorsed its main conclusion: 53% believed that racial IQ differences had a genetic foundation at least in part.

I remain unconvinced that racial IQ differences are genetic in origin, or that these differences can be equated with intelligence differences. Setting aside the question of the relationship between IQ and intelligence for later, my first task is to make a prima facie case that an environmental explanation of IQ differences is viable. Since I have had my say about Black and White elsewhere (Flynn, 1980, 1987b, 1989), this book discusses only Sino-Japanese and Whites.

THE VIABILITY OF ENVIRONMENTALISM

There are several considerations supposed to render environmentalism powerless to explain IQ differences between Chinese or Japanese on the one hand, and White Americans on the other. The overall IQ difference is between 1 and 5 points and the latter is a sizable difference amounting to one-third of a standard deviation; the discrepancy between nonverbal and verbal IQ, when Japanese are normed on White Americans, is even greater, amounting to 14 points. Moreover, textbook environmental factors such as SES offer no explanation and the fact that the Japanese gain against Whites as they mature forces the environmentalist into convoluted hypotheses, such as that a poor Japanese environment for young children evolves into a superior one for adolescents. I can dismiss the maturity point quickly by anticipating some of our American data. The Coleman Report covers grades 1 to 12 and gives us a picture of Chinese and Japanese growing up in America. In America, at least, it was the youngest children who had the highest IQs, indeed, Chinese and Japanese first graders outscored Chinese and Japanese high school students for both nonverbal and overall IQ (see Table 2.3). The other points call for detailed treatment as follows.

Overall IQ Differences

Generational data show that unknown environmental factors can cause huge IQ differences between groups. Flynn (1987a) showed that young adults in 1980 outscored the young adults of 1950 in 14 nations, ranging from Europe to the Commonwealth to America to Japan, with an average difference of 15 points. This phenomenon is of particular interest because the differences are known to be environmental in origin and yet, textbook environmental factors are as powerless here as they are in explaining IQ differences between nations. For example, the Dutch gained 20 IQ points between 1952 and 1982 with the rate of gain escalating during that period. The advent of test sophistication may have had an initial impact of a few points, but such gains fade away rapidly and cannot explain an escalating rate of gain. Increased years of schooling accounted for only 1 IQ point and enhanced SES accounted for only 3 points, leaving a huge residue caused by unknown environmental factors. The Dutch gains were verified by a direct comparison of sons with their own fathers, so we know that genetic factors played virtually no role.

Someday we will identify the environmental factors at work in generational IQ gains and they may not prove exotic or unfamiliar. However, it is their enormous and unexpected potency that is so baffling. When Archimedes wanted to impress Hiero with the power of the lever, he took a ship in drydock, heavy laden with many passengers and freight, and clasping the end of a compound pulley drew her along smoothly as if moving under full sail at sea. It would be uninformative to say Archimedes was using something familiar, his muscles, because without knowledge of the principle of the lever, what he could do with his muscles was quite inexplicable. If environmental factors show unanticipated potency, at least in advanced societies, we must look at the environment with new eyes and try to identify the unknown forces that have done so much to transform the factors we know. The Dutch of 1982 outscored the Dutch of 1972 by 8 IQ points. Arguably the cultural distance between those two groups, 10 years of cultural evolution within the Netherlands, is less than the cultural distance separating China or Japan from White America. Until we know what happened, and can show that generational-type factors do not operate between nations, it would be premature to assume that environmental differences cannot account for national differences of 1 to 5 IQ points.

Nonverbal Versus Verbal Differences

The fact that the discrepancy between Japanese performance IQ and verbal IQ, when they are normed on White Americans, amounts to fully 14 points appears to pose a more difficult problem. In 1987, Flynn (1987c) responded to Lynn's challenge to show that environmental factors had the potency to cause such a discrepancy. He conceded the magnitude of the difference. There is no doubt that the Japanese WISC-R sample easily outscored White Americans for performance IQ, with their scores on the Block Design and Object Assembly subtests being particularly significant as evidence of visuospatial ability. There is no doubt that the Japanese sample did worse than Americans for verbal IQ, thanks to low scores on Comprehension and Digit Span.

Moreover, other scholars, such as Kaufman, McLean, Ishikuma, and Moon (1986), have reinforced Lynn's case that the Japanese brain was lateralized differently than the American brain. First, they endorsed Lynn's contention that the discrepancy between performance and verbal IQ could mean that the right hemisphere of the Japanese brain had made gains at the expense of the left hemisphere. Second, they pointed out that the right hemisphere is the locus of simultaneous processing, the ability to solve highly integrated problems often spatial or analogical in character. On the other hand, the left hemisphere is the locus of sequential processing, solving problems that require step-by-step handling of elements that have a linear or temporal relationship with one another. And third, as far as the WISC-R was concerned, they designated Block Design and Object Assembly as the primary measures of simultaneous processing, Comprehension and Digit Span as the sole measures of sequential processing.

Once again the generational IQ data show that environmental factors have the potency to account for these differences.   Table 1.2 compares between-

TABLE 1.2

Ability differences that separate both generations and nations

Performance-verbal differences

	Between-generations[a]					Between-nations[b]
	America	Japan	Austria	Germany	France	Japan/America
Performance	10	22	28	28	19	11
Verbal	8	20	20	12	3	–3
P–V[c]	2	2	8	16	16	14

[a]The IQ advantages ($SD = 15$) of contemporary children over children 30 years ago in various nations. [b]The IQ advantage of Japanese children over White Americans, 1975, Japanese sample unaltered—from Table 1.1, column III. [c]Performance differences minus verbal differences.

Simultaneous-sequential processing differences

		Between-generations[a]		Between-nations[b]
		Austria	Germany	Japan/America
Simultaneous subtests	Block design	+3.2	+5.4	+3.8
	Object assembly	+1.7	+2.7	+0.7
Sequential subtests	Digit span	–0.5	+0.6	+0.5
	Comprehension	+0.1	+2.6	–2.0

[a]The scaled-score advantages ($SD = 3$) of contemporary children over children 30 years ago in various nations. [b]The scaled-score advantage of the Japanese WISC-R sample over the American WISC-R sample, White members only.

Sources: Flynn, 1987a, Table 17; Lynn & Hampson, 1986, Table 3; Schallberger, 1985, Table 4; Schubert & Berlach, 1982, Table 2. The Wechsler subtest gains have been projected over 30 years. For example, Schallberger gives a 4.85 scaled-score gain for Block Design for a period of 27 years: 4.85 ÷ 27 = .180; that x 30 = 5.4.

generations ability differences with the national differences between Japan and America. It is immediately apparent that there is nothing extraordinary about the 14 points that separate performance and verbal IQ when Japan is compared to America. In both West Germany and France, 16 points separate performance and verbal IQ when this generation is compared to the last. Concerning the Japanese simultaneous versus sequential processing gap, compared to White Americans, the relevant subtest data were available between generations only for Austria and West Germany. In those nations, the this generation/last generation results mimic the Japan/America results. The West German score for Comprehension may seem to be too high but the absolute values are not the point. The relevant pattern is that simultaneous subtest scores are higher than sequential test scores. Also Comprehension makes considerably less contribution to sequential processing than does Digit Span, so in fact the between-generations results match the between-nations results almost perfectly.

IQ differences between Japan and America may have nothing to do with whether the Japanese brain is lateralized differently from the American brain. It is possible that the brains of German speakers have relateralized over the last 30 years but it seems unlikely. Evolution has had little opportunity to influence genes over that time and the German language has not undergone radical change, that is, vowel sounds have not gone from a frequency akin to English toward a frequency akin to Japanese. The causes of test score differences between Japanese and White Americans may well be environmental factors and factors far more prosaic than those suggested by brain physiology or linguistics.

Evidence Specific to China and Japan

Thus far the defense of the viability of environmentalism has been general with only analogical relevance to IQ differences between China or Japan and White America. The environmental factors that create IQ differences between generations may exist between those nations but, then again, they may not. If existent they may work against Whites but, then again, they may work against Chinese or Japanese. But imagine that the IQ differences between all these races tended to disappear as they approached being raised in a common environment. Assume that Chinese and Japanese Americans, Chinese and Japanese born or reared in the United States or both, developed lower verbal IQs than White Americans, no higher nonverbal IQs, and lower overall IQs. Assume that a broader array of data suggested that visuospatial ability does little to explain group achievement in modern America. Then we would have highly specific evidence with direct relevance.

The notion that Chinese and Japanese Americans suffer from IQ deficits may seem too unlikely to merit serious consideration. The literature is full of the extraordinary achievements of Asian Americans, and high achievement and high IQ normally go together. Therefore, we turn our attention to that literature, which means turning away from the world scene toward the American scene. A word before we go concerning evolutionary theory. Lynn's evolutionary scenario has plausible features and it would be possible to add theories equally plausible. During much of the Christian era, the clergy in European countries may have been both an intellectual elite and celibate. Over many generations, this would tend to cause a genetic deficit for intelligence for Whites as compared to Sino-Japanese. But the plausibility of an evolutionary theory is secondary to whether it is needed at all. The whole mechanics of evolution is natural selection operating on genes and if genetic differences cause only minor between-race trait differences, the role of evolutionary theory is circumscribed. This is not to say that any contribution to causal explanation is to be despised. It is merely to say that theories solve existent and not nonexistent causal problems.

THE AMERICAN NATURAL ARISTOCRACY

Almost 25 years ago, Weyl (1966) appraised what he called "the American natural aristocracy" and concluded that Chinese and Japanese played an outstanding role. He confirmed this in his classic analysis of the 1960 census (Weyl, 1969). Chinese Americans had three to five times their proportionate share of college faculty, architects, scientists, school teachers, engineers, and physicians, and fell behind Whites only where political connections count, lawyers and judges, and in subprofessions like nursing and the clergy. Japanese Americans excelled in the same fields, although to a lesser degree, and had twice their proportionate share of artists and writers. Weyl gave his own evolutionary scenario for the positive selection of Chinese for intelligence, competitive exams throughout Chinese history created an intellectual elite who had plural wives and more offspring, and predicted that the future achievements of Chinese and Japanese Americans would be even greater.

The children of Weyl's subjects plus newly arrived Asian Americans confirmed his prediction. During the 1970s and 1980s, Asian Americans virtually matched White performance on the Scholastic Aptitude Test (SAT) despite the fact that a much higher percentage took the test: for example, in 1985, the upper 70% of Asian 18-year-olds took the SAT and matched the upper 27% of Whites, lower on the verbal test but higher on the mathematics test (ETS, 1985, 1988). Asian Americans entered and graduated from universities in unprecedented numbers: the 1980 census showed that 35% of Asian adults had college degrees as compared to 17% of Whites. Between 1981 and 1987, Asian American high school students were much overrepresented among winners of National Merit Scholarships, U.S. Presidential Scholarships, Arts Recognition and Talent Search scholars, and Westinghouse Science Talent Search scholars. This last, America's most prestigious high school science competition, had 20 Asian winners out of the 70 chosen over those 7 years, indeed, in 1986, the top five winners were all Asian Americans.

During the 1980s, there was an explosion of articles about Asian Americans in publications like *The New York Times, U.S. News and World Report, Time, USA Today, The New Republic,* and *Time* once again. Their numbers at prestige universities had made a powerful impression on the popular imagination. Asian Americans were just over 2% of the population and yet, the 1984 entering class had 9% Asians at Princeton, 11% at Harvard and Stanford, 19% at the California Institute of Technology and Berkeley. By 1987, the percentages were even higher, 14% at Harvard, 16% at Stanford, 20% at the Massachusettes Institute of Technology, 21% at Cal Tech, 25% at Berkeley, and this despite accusations that admissions quotas had been introduced to limit their numbers. The famed Juilliard School of Music has consistently had a student body 25% Asian. The percentages are not as impressive as they look: some Asian entrants into elite universities are recent arrivals whose high school education was abroad and some do not intend to remain in America. Nonetheless, the majority are American born or American educated and they still constitute a flood that puts them well ahead of other ethnic groups. These high achievers are not all Chinese and Japanese, of course. The Asian American community has expanded over the last 20 years to include a wide range of subgroups, but Chinese and Japanese figure prominently, as do fast-growing groups such as Indians (from India) and Koreans (Bell, 1985; Brand, 1987; Doerner, 1985; Gardner, Robey, & Smith, 1985; Greenwald, 1985; Hsia, 1988; Kanengiser, 1985; Lindsey, 1982; McBee, 1984).

When journalists approached Arthur Jensen for an explanation, he endorsed the view that Asian Americans do so well because they are smarter, citing several IQ studies of Chinese Americans (Brand, 1987, pp. 44-45). However, the real foundation of belief in the high IQs of Chinese and Japanese Americans lies elsewhere: Vernon's great book *The Abilities and Achievements of Orientals in North America.*

VERNON AND CHINESE IQ

Without exception, scholars cite Vernon's overall assessment of the IQ testing of Chinese American children between 1918 and 1980. Vernon (1982, p. 28) said that right from the 1920s, Chinese American children scored lower than Whites on verbal tests but equal or higher on nonverbal tests. He also noted a trend: the verbal deficit used to be quite considerable, but recent studies put Chinese American verbal IQ at 97, little below the White average; and recent studies put their nonverbal IQ at 110, well above the White average. It is clear that the recent studies Vernon had in mind are these: Jensen's testing of children from San Francisco's Chinatown, done in 1975, which gave them a verbal IQ of 97 and a nonverbal IQ of 110 on the Lorge-Thorndike Intelligence Test; and a study by Jensen and Inouye of the Berkeley, California public schools which yielded a sample about 70% Chinese and 30% Japanese with very high Lorge-Thorndike IQs. Vernon discounted the Berkeley results somewhat, due to the elite character of the school district, but believed that they reinforced the Chinatown results.

My own cursory survey of studies done through the mid-1960s was less favorable to Chinese Americans than Vernon's, suggesting no better than parity with Whites for nonverbal IQ. But mainly, my suspicions were aroused by the two recent studies on which he put such great weight. I knew from personal correspondence with Jensen that the Berkeley study had actually been done in 1968 and wondered if Vernon had thought it done circa 1980. A 10-point rise in Chinese nonverbal IQ (from 100 to 110) between 1965 and 1980 was unlikely, but such a rise between 1965 and 1968 was quite incredible. Moreover, when the elite Chinese of Berkeley were compared to the elite Whites of Berkeley, the Chinese actually had somewhat lower IQs. And the IQ values for both races looked odd, for example, Berkeley Whites had 118 for verbal IQ and 120 for nonverbal IQ: no school district in America should have an average IQ that high, however elite it might be.

I began to suspect that the Berkeley IQs had been inflated by the fact that the Lorge-Thorndike test norms were obsolete. If the test had been normed not in 1968, when the children were tested, but say back in 1953, the Berkeley children were being scored against, not a representative sample of contemporary children, but a sample 15 years out of date. As we have seen, there have been massive IQ gains over time, so to score the children of today against those of 15 years ago is to score against a substandard sample. And this cast doubt on the results of the Chinatown study: if Berkeley children tested in 1968 had inflated IQs because of obsolete Lorge-Thorndike norms, the Chinatown children of 1975 would have IQs even more inflated.

Therefore, there is good reason to review Vernon's data and ask whether or not he might have been mistaken. And if Vernon was mistaken, we need a whole new pair of spectacles. Up to now, high IQ and high achievement seemed to reinforce one another as evidence of the superior intelligence of Chinese and Japanese Americans. But if their mean IQ is no higher than Whites, or even below Whites, then their ordinary IQs and extraordinary achievements would give conflicting evidence. We would be forced to choose between their IQ and achievements as a measure of their intelligence: the latter entails the concession that IQ tests are deceptive when used to compare Chinese and Japanese and White Americans for intelligence; the former entails the concession that nonintelligence factors often outweigh intelligence as determinants of group achievement. Even if we reserved judgment about whether IQ tests measure intelligence, the brute facts would dictate that **non-IQ** factors have a potent role in group achievement. That in itself has important implications not only for Chinese and Japanese Americans, but also for ethnic groups such as Blacks and Filipinos, gender groups (I refer to women and their underachievement in mathematics), and nations, for example, America's attitude to Japan's economic performance. A problem that seemed rather humdrum (they do so well because they are smarter) suddenly poses a challenge to the intellect.

ORGANIZATION AND CONTENTS

Much of the remainder of this book is a detailed analysis of the IQ and achievements of Chinese and Japanese Americans. The data available dictate emphasis on those who were born in America or migrated to America prior to 1970, ideally, prior to 1968. The remaining chapters have the following contents: Chapters 2 and 3 analyze the IQ literature both national surveys and local studies; Chapter 4 offers estimates of the mean IQs of Chinese and Japanese Americans and attempts to measure the disparity between their IQ and their achievements; Chapter 5 dissects the process whereby Chinese and Japanese Americans overachieve; Chapter 6 issues a brief caveat; Chapter 7 returns to the subject of superior genes, emphasizes the non-IQ factors that influence group achievement, and exemplifies those factors by a comparison of Chinese with Irish with Black Americans. Chapter 8 is a short epilogue that ends with a celebration of the contribution Chinese and Japanese Americans have made to American life.

2

The Three Great
National Surveys

Our intent is to discuss all IQ studies whose subjects have included Chinese or Japanese Americans. This chapter gives some attention to early studies and a detailed analysis of the three great national surveys of the 1960s. Studies analyzed rather than merely summarized are prefaced with a diagnosis of whether or not the values for Chinese or Japanese IQ have been inflated. Often the inflated values are simply what an uncritical reading of the data would give and therefore, they must not be taken as an indictment of the scholars concerned. Sometimes these scholars had other purposes in mind and offered no IQ estimates; sometimes they offered estimates but could not possibly have realized they were using obsolete norms. All inflated estimates are revised downward, which should not be taken as an indictment of the analysis. Just as rising prices over time mean the value of currency is always being inflated, so IQ gains over time mean that IQ scores are always being inflated. When subjects are scored against obsolete norms, the only way to revise is downward.

Comparative studies of Asian and White American IQ fall naturally into four periods, namely, 1918 to 1949, 1950 to 1971, 1972 to 1975, and 1976 to 1985. The subjects chosen, the tests administered, and the methodology used were conditioned by the ebb and flow of immigration, which Asian groups were most tolerated or acculturated, even the terminology scholars adopted at the time. Without some knowledge of these developments, the studies cannot be properly assessed and therefore, a historical interlude prefaces each period.

EXCLUSION AND RELOCATION: 1918-1949

The focus of scholarly interest in these years was the group called "Orientals", a term now abandoned as pejorative but in dominant use until quite recently. Having no desire to resurrect the term, I use it only when necessary, that is, when indispensable in describing the subjects of past studies. The groups that answered to this label were almost entirely Chinese, Japanese, and Korean and since Koreans constituted at that time only 2% of the Oriental population, they were neglected.

Chinese had come to America as far back as 1848, but efforts to normalize their situation were impeded by bias and restrictive legislation. They were overwhelmingly male and, between 1924 and 1946, they could secure entry for their minor children but not their wives. Early IQ studies of Chinese children may include some separated from their mothers with the exception of those done in Hawaii where established families were more common. Japanese immigration did not begin until 1884, but many brought wives with them before restrictive legislation took effect and therefore, they enjoyed a normal family life. The Nisei or second generation became high achievers in American schools beginning about 1930. However, in 1942, West Coast Japanese, who were about 45% of the total population, suffered the trauma of war-time evacuation into relocation centers (Grodzins, 1949).

EARLY STUDIES

Vernon (1982, pp. 17-19, 70, 89-95, and 160) collected 18 studies in which Chinese or Japanese or both were compared to Whites, all subjects tested sometime between 1918 and 1935. Setting aside Luh and Wu (1931) who described their sample as elite and two small samples of university students (Porteus & Babcock, 1926; Wang, 1926), who of course would have been highly selected, 15 studies remain. None of these are worth analyzing in detail, all are deficient in terms of information given, test quality, or sample quality, but they do convey an overall impression.

There were five studies with verbal tests only, three with nonverbal tests only, and seven with both, which collectively give 12 verbal comparisons and 10 nonverbal comparisons. Whites scored higher on all verbal tests, usually much higher, although Chinese came close to parity on one. The results on nonverbal tests were evenly divided, showing Whites higher in four studies (Japanese are almost equal in one of these), lower in four studies (Japanese are only equal in one of these), and equal in the remaining two. There is a tendency for Whites to do better on the more complex nonverbal tests and worse on tests like Goodenough's Draw-a-Man or purely memory tests. Nonetheless, a pattern of Chinese and Japanese Americans having lower verbal IQs than Whites, but parity on nonverbal tests, is foreshadowed even in these early studies.

HONOLULU 1938

Estimates: Taken together, Chinese and Japanese get 99 for nonverbal IQ, 86 for verbal IQ. Adjustments: None, because scored against a contemporary and reasonably representative sample of local Whites.

Smith (1942) tested children aged 10 to 14 years in the Honolulu public schools during the spring of 1938. Whites, Chinese, and Japanese were distinguished from children of mixed race and Whites did not include either Puerto Ricans or Portuguese. In Hawaii, Portuguese originally constituted a separate ethnic group. All Whites were tested but due to the great number of Chinese and Japanese less than half of them were selected, by a method using the initial letter of their surnames. A comprehensive testing in 1924 had shown that this method introduced no bias. In passing, the results of that 1924 study are useless for our purposes because at that time, few Whites patronized the public schools. Smith used a nonverbal test with several subtests: geometrical shapes that posed oddity problems and served as a measure of fluid intelligence; a mazes subtest; and dot imitation, mainly a test of visual acuity and short-term memory. He used two verbal tests, called spoken English and printed English, but really tests of general information, comprehension, and vocabulary.

Smith presented raw score means and standard deviations and these have been used to convert his results into deviation IQ scores. Since both sexes and all ages were well represented, the raw score values were simply averaged rather than a weighted average calculated, a procedure I follow throughout. The Chinese or Japanese raw score mean was subtracted from the White mean, the difference divided by the White raw score SD, and the White IQ mean and SD set at 100 and 15 respectively. This has the advantage that scores need be presented only for Asian subjects, Whites always having by definition a mean IQ of 100, and this procedure is also followed throughout. There was one exception to use of the White raw score SD : Whites found the spoken English test too easy and a ceiling effect both depressed their mean and attenuated their variance; therefore, the Japanese SD was used. Table 2.1 gives an example of how nonverbal IQ scores were calculated. IQ scores were calculated in the same way for the spoken and printed English tests and then averaged to get the verbal IQ. The overall IQ is simply the average of the verbal and nonverbal scores, paving the way for comparison with full scale IQ from other studies.

TABLE 2.1
Honolulu 1938: Mean IQ of Chinese and Japanese schoolchildren

Race	Age (years)	N	IQ		
			Nonverbal	Verbal	Overall
Chinese	10–12	799	99.04	86.96	93.00
	13–14	553	96.30	91.55	93.92
	10–14	1352	97.95	88.72	93.34
Japanese	10–12	1007	101.93	82.27	92.10
	13–14	649	99.44	85.94	92.69
	10–14	1656	100.92	83.68	92.30
Both	10–12	1806	100.49	84.62	92.55
	13–14	1202	97.87	88.75	93.31
	10–14	3008	99.44	86.20	92.82

Example of calculations:

(1) Chinese raw score mean on nonverbal test, the average of both sexes and all ages 10–12 = 40.495; (2) White mean = 41.075, White SD = 9.042; (3) 40.495 – 41.075 = – 0.58, that ÷ 9.042 = –.064 $SDU;$ (4) White IQ mean = 100, White IQ SD = 15; (5) –.064 x 15 = –0.96, that + 100 = **99.04** as Chinese IQ mean on nonverbal test.

Taking Chinese and Japanese together, Table 2.1 gives a nonverbal IQ of about 99, a verbal IQ of 86, and an overall IQ of 93. Japanese score 3 points above Chinese for nonverbal, 5 points below for verbal, but these differences disappear in later data. Later studies also show both groups making significant verbal IQ gains on Whites, but the 1938 nonverbal score of 99.44 is never exceeded. However, this score may be deceptive in that Smith's White children were almost certainly substandard to some degree. His own data show that in 1924, White children in the Honolulu public schools were 11 to 14 IQ points below mainland Whites. By 1938, an influx of mainland Whites plus better White patronage of improved public schools had done something to close the gap (Smith, 1942, pp. 67-68). Nonetheless, Smith's public school sample included only 52% of the White school population which means, allowing for a few absentees, that 45% were in private schools. These percentages include Puerto Ricans and Portuguese among Whites (Bureau of the Census, 1940, Hawaii, Table 5) and therefore, the percentage of "mainstream" Whites in private schools was undoubtedly much higher.

If mainstream Whites circa 1938 were substandard by say 3 points in the Honolulu public schools, Chinese and Japanese at that time really had mean

IQs of 96 to 97 nonverbal, about 83 verbal, and about 90 overall. These values would leave room for subsequent improvement on all tests.

WYOMING 1943-1945

Estimate: Japanese get 96 for verbal IQ. Adjustments: No major adjustments because California Japanese scored against a contemporary sample of Wyoming Whites.

Portenier (1947) took advantage of the fact that 10,000 Japanese Americans were interred from 1943 to 1945 at the Heart Mountain Relocation Project. This was located at Cody, Wyoming and at that time, the University of Wyoming tested seniors (the 12th grade) in all Wyoming high schools, using the Ohio State University Psychological Test, Form 21. Portenier isolated the scores of the Heart Mountain seniors for comparison with the total statewide results for the years 1943, 1944, and 1945. She also reported results from a special testing program at Heart Mountain using the Henmon-Nelson Tests of Mental Ability and the Terman-McNemar Test of Mental Ability, although only for 1945. Here the only basis for comparison is between the Japanese scores and the test norms. The Ohio State Test is entirely verbal, that is, vocabulary using same and opposites, reasoning using analogies, and reading comprehension (Pinter, 1938, p. 105). The Terman-McNemar Test is very similar and also entirely verbal, the Henmon-Nelson mainly so (Easley, 1941, p. 222; Hovland, 1949, p. 342). The Japanese were mainly from California and those tested were 1% Issei or foreign born, 91% Nisei or second generation and American born, and 8% Sansei or third generation.

For the Ohio State Test, Portenier gave raw score means and *SDs* for 1945 and sufficient data on the distributions for 1943 and 1944 to allow means to be derived. Therefore, these could be translated into deviation IQs as already described. Since the Japanese scores are included in the all-Wyoming results, they must be removed to get a comparison between Japanese and all other subjects. Moreover, Wyoming at that time had a small minority of Blacks and Indians, about 1.6%, and I have assumed that 1% of high school seniors were minority students with an IQ one standard deviation below the White mean. However, these two adjustments make a difference of only half an IQ point. For the Henmon-Nelson Test, she gave percentile comparisons between the Japanese curve and the test norms and for the Terman-McNemar, she noted that 25% of the Japanese were above the test-norm average. Therefore, a table for areas under a normal curve allows us to calculate the difference in standard deviations between the Japanese mean and the normative sample mean.

TABLE 2.2
Wyoming 1943 to 1945: Mean IQ of Japanese, 12th Grade

Date	N	Ohio State University	Henmon-Nelson	Terman-McNemar
			Tests	
1943	192	95.40	–	–
1944	251	95.41	–	–
1945	226	96.34	89.14	89.88

Table 2.2 presents results for all three tests. In 1943-1945, Japanese 12th graders averaged just under 96 for verbal IQ on the Ohio State Test, the other tests giving values of 89 to 90.   Normally, the Ohio State results would be preferred. The Terman-McNemar norms were of reasonable quality (Hovland, 1949, p. 342) but an IQ estimate based on one point of comparison is suspect.   As for the Henmon-Nelson, the norms were suspect. They were updated every two years on the basis of asking test users to mail in results but as Fowler (1953, p. 399) pointed out, this hardly substitutes for a carefully selected standardization sample, particularly when no information is presented about stratification variables. In contrast, the Ohio State Test gave a precise IQ estimate and the Japanese subjects were scored against all Wyoming High School seniors, a contemporaneous sample from a reasonably large and typical state. There is evidence that Wyoming seniors were a good match for those from another large and typical state, namely, Ohio. The Wyoming median in 1945 was at the Ohio 55th percentile which gives an advantage of 1.9 IQ points.   The Ohio State Test, Form 21, was normed in 1940 (Ohio State, 1949, p. 323) and assuming gains over time at the rate of .3 IQ points per year (Flynn, 1984b), the predicted advantage would be 1.5 IQ points (5 years x .3 = 1.5).

Having argued for the Ohio State Test results, which give a Japanese verbal IQ of 96 in 1943-1945, I must concede that they pose a serious problem.   The Honolulu Japanese of 1938 aged 10 to 12 years would have been 17 years old in 1943-1945 and yet, their verbal IQ was only 82 (Table 2.1). It is true that older schoolchildren scored 86, but that still leaves a 10-point difference. It seems unlikely that the Californian Japanese interred at Heart Mountain were that much ahead of Hawaiian Japanese. Portenier (1947, p. 57) opined that Japanese who were inferior students were mostly dropped from school at Heart Mountain by the 12th grade. But this would inflate the mean IQ of the Japanese tested only if fewer White students dropped out of school by the 12th grade. Perhaps conditions at Heart

Mountain encouraged a higher Japanese attrition rate but in the absence of actual data, I have assumed the rates were similar. Under normal conditions, more Whites than Japanese would leave high school before graduation.

The problems posed by these older studies should not distract us from the main drift. Even if the highest values from both Honolulu and Wyoming are selected for emphasis, Chinese would have a nonverbal IQ of 98 and Japanese 101; neither would have a verbal IQ above 96. Since these values are close to later values, their selection would merely mean that Chinese and Japanese had made up most of their verbal IQ deficit by 1945 and made no significant gains over the next generation.

ACCULTURATION AND PROGRESS: 1950-1971

By 1960, there were 240,000 Chinese Americans about 75% of whom were U.S. citizens, the rest being resident aliens or visitors, primarily businessmen or students. Those born in America after 1950 regarded themselves as Americans and had rarely experienced serious discrimination. By 1965, over 75% of the school population, ages 5 to 19 years, were American born and Chinese had equalled Whites in years of education. Japanese Americans numbered 460,000, the school population was 93% American born, and they had surpassed Whites in years of education. The dominant group was the Sansei or third generation and they were highly acculturated, that is, they were confident of their ability to succeed in White society and proud of their ethnic identity (Gardner, Robey, & Smith, 1985, p. 14; Vernon, 1982, pp. 7-16 and 42-44).

This period was the final phase of the original Chinese and Japanese American communities as they were from their inception up through the mid-1960s. Soon they were to be joined by a wave of new immigrants but, fortunately, before that occurred another eight studies were completed. Three of these comprise the only national surveys ever done of Asian American IQ.

THE COLEMAN REPORT

Estimates: Chinese and Japanese 12th graders get 100 for nonverbal IQ, 97 for verbal IQ; grades 3 to 12 average a point or two less. Adjustments: No major adjustments because scored against a contemporary and representative sample of White Americans.

In 1965, J.S. Coleman and his associates aimed at a 5% sample of all pupils in America's public schools. They divided the nation into metropolitan areas and counties outside metropolitan areas, selected 66 areas and 332 counties, and from these selected 1170 high schools. At each step, they used random methods, but within limits set by the need to obtain numbers of nonwhite subjects large enough for statistical purposes. For each high school selected, they identified the elementary schools which fed students into that high school which gave a total of 3,223 elementary schools. Eventually, 780 high schools and 2,377 elementary schools supplied student test results and questionnaires; they make a strong case that the nonrespondent schools were not atypical in any significant way (Coleman et al., 1966a, pp. 550-572).

All pupils were tested at grades 12, 9, 6, and 3 and a randomly selected half at Grade 1. This gave them a pool of 568,743 subjects tested and processed. From this pool, they selected a sample of 8,000 Whites at each of the five grade levels, a sample of almost 1,000 "Orientals" at each level, and so forth for other ethnic groups. These samples were used to calculate all test results. Thanks to weighting equations, they simulate random samples from the nation's public school population. That is, each White subject in the pool had a chance of being selected in proportion to the number of pupils in the White school population he or she represented, the same for each Oriental subject, and so forth. The use of the term Oriental was fortuitous in producing a sample that would be almost entirely Japanese and Chinese, about 64% Japanese, 34% Chinese, and 2% mainly Korean and those Filipinos who consider themselves ethnically Chinese. Mayeske (personal communication, October 8, 1987) and his colleague Okada confirmed that only a few Filipinos, those of "Oriental appearance", would classify themselves as such. Mayeske was senior author of the follow-up analyses of the Coleman Report. At my request, Jensen (personal communication, September 15, 1987) consulted a knowledgeable member of the California Filipino community who was emphatically of the same opinion.

They administered nonverbal and verbal IQ tests at all grade levels and, at all levels above Grade 1, academic achievement tests in reading comprehension and mathematics. The nonverbal tests used shapes to set classification and analogy problems, the verbal tests used sentence completion and synonyms and were drawn from the School and College Ability Tests (SCAT) series. The reading comprehension tests presented passages of prose and poetry with emphasis on interpretation and drawing inferences, the mathematics tests emphasized problem solving rather than computation (Coleman et al., 1966a, pp. 575-584). A general information test was administered at grades 9 and 12, but its results were so close to the reading test that I have omitted them.

A Supplementary Appendix gives raw score means and *SDs* (Coleman et al., 1966b) and deviation IQs were calculated for all tests at all levels. There

TABLE 2.3

Coleman Report: Mean IQ and Achievement Test Scores of Orientals[a]

Grade	N	IQ			Achievement		
		Nonverbal	Verbal	Overall	Math	Reading	Overall
1	999	104.03	96.99	100.51	–	–	–
3	999	97.59	93.90	95.75	95.80	95.75	95.77
6	998	95.50	93.63	94.56	94.23	94.92	94.58
9	999	101.16	95.80	98.48	99.38	97.10	98.24
12	999	100.25	96.70	98.48	99.77	95.62	97.70
3–12	3995	98.63	95.01	96.82	97.30	95.85	96.57

[a]All scores for grade 12 raised by .88 points to compensate for differential attrition at that level—see text. That adjustment raises the average scores for grades 3–12 by .22 points. Calculations based on census data and probable values give similar results—see below.

I. Key values for calculations: (1) Percentage attrition by 12th grade, Chinese & Japanese = 7.5%, White (minus Hispanics) = 15% (Bureau of the Census, 1970, DC:US, Table 197; Bureau of the Census, 1970, PC(2)–1G, Tables 3 & 18; Coleman et al., 1966a, p. 450, Table 6.1.3); (2) Correlation between IQ and years of schooling = .60 (Jensen, 1980, p. 334); (3) Oriental *SDs,* nonverbal = 18.07, verbal = 15.41—see text.

II. Calculation of adjusted nonverbal mean: (1) Bottom 7.5% of Orientals missing, mean raised by .1443 *SDU;* (2) .1443 x 18.07 *(SD)* x .60 (correlation) = mean raised by 1.57 IQ points; (3) Bottom 15% of Whites missing, mean raised by .274 *SDU;* (4) .274 x 15 *(SD)* x .60 (correlation) = mean raised by 2.47 IQ points; (5) 2.47 - 1.57 = .90 IQ points as Oriental disadvantage; (6) 99.37 (unadjusted mean) + .90 = 100.27 as adjusted mean.

III. Calculation of adjusted verbal mean: (1) Using Oriental *SD* = 15.41 gives 1.13 IQ points as Oriental disadvantage; (2) 95.82 (unadjusted mean) + 1.13 = 96.95 as adjusted mean.

is one necessary adjustment to the Coleman Report results: census data show that until after the school leaving age of 16, school attendance was virtually universal among all ethnic groups; but by the 12th grade, 7.5% of Chinese plus Japanese and 15% of Whites minus Hispanics were missing. This means that Oriental 12th graders were less elite than White 12th graders and theoretical calculations show that this would lower Oriental IQ by about one point (see the bottom of Table 2.3). This almost exactly matches the .88 IQ points Orientals lost between the 9th and 12th grades and therefore, I have used that value to adjust: the "missing" .88 points have been added to all 12th grade mean IQ and achievement test scores. As for *SDs*, the 9th grade values would be unaffected by differential attrition of Orientals and Whites and should be used at the 12th grade as well. The match between theory and "reality" may of course be fortuitous. No single stratified sample of 1,000 subjects can be assumed accurate within one IQ point.

Table 2.3 averages grades 3 to 12 so as to get results from a sample of almost 4,000 Oriental subjects. These show Chinese and Japanese Americans circa 1965 at 99 for nonverbal, 95 for verbal, and 97 for overall IQ. However, throughout most of this book, I use not these but the slightly higher values from the Coleman Report 12th graders. It is better to err on the side of caution with imperfect data. Moreover, the 12th graders are the right age to provide a good match with occupational data from the 1980 census, something that will concern us greatly later on. Therefore, the Coleman Report values utilized will be: mean IQ, 100 for nonverbal, 97 for verbal, and 98.5 for overall; IQ variance, 18.07 for nonverbal *SD* and 15.41 for verbal *SD* . These give an average of 16.74 as *SD* for overall IQ, a value which assumes that the correlation between nonverbal and verbal IQ is similar for Orientals and Whites.

Table 2.3 shows a close match between Oriental IQ and achievement scores but it is important to note the content of the tests here classified as achievement. The Coleman Report reading comprehension and general information tests are not unlike the Comprehension and Information subtests of the Wechsler verbal IQ scale. The mathematics tests, although undoubtedly requiring some knowledge, test general problem-solving skills far more than the content of school-taught mathematics courses.

PROJECT TALENT

Estimates: Chinese and Japanese get 97 for nonverbal IQ, 96 for verbal IQ. Adjustments: No major adjustments because scored against contemporary White Americans and no way of assessing follow-up sample bias.

In 1960, J.C. Flanagan and his associates took a 5% sample which represented a stratified random sample of American high schools. Although not identical, their methods were similar enough to the Coleman Report to guarantee an initial sample of good quality, the major difference being that they sampled private and parochial schools as well as public (Flanagan et al., 1962, pp. 43-56). They administered a wide variety of tests to 88,000 12th grade students and in 1965, five years later, 24,000 of those tested responded to a follow-up questionnaire and gave information about their ethnicity (Flanagan & Cooley, 1966).

About 91.8% of respondents classified themselves as White and 0.7% as Oriental (essentially Chinese and Japanese) with both groups slightly overrepresented. Whites were divided into Jewish and non-Jewish and the latter included Hispanics. The large number of respondents who were non-Jewish White was reduced by taking a 5% sample. Backman (1972) deleted a few subjects from all groups who were at the very top and bottom of the socioeconomic scale, but this should not have had any differential effect on Whites and Orientals. The final pool of 2,925 subjects had 1,051 non-Jewish Whites, 150 Orientals, 1,256 Jewish Whites, and 488 Blacks.

Backman (1972, pp. 2-3 and 6) presented scores for Whites and Orientals that pose a few problems, minor problems fortunately. First, she translated raw scores into standard scores based on the original Project Talent sample with its SD set at 10. This is virtually equivalent to our translation of raw scores into deviation IQs, but we must adjust for the fact that the original sample included all races rather than Whites only. Since the ratio between an all races SD and a White SD is typically 15 to 14, simple arithmetic converts the distance between the White and Oriental means into White SDs (Flynn, 1984b, p. 31). Set the White mean at 100 and SD at 15 and there results our usual deviation IQ scores. Second, the sample consisted of 12th graders and, as we saw under the Coleman Report, Orientals would be less elite than Whites at that level and deserve .88 points as compensation. Third, the Whites included about 3.3% Hispanics. Since their mean IQ tends to be about 14 points below other Whites, they would have pulled down the White mean and the Whites deserve .48 points as compensation. These adjustments have been made, but they are minor and collectively add only .40 points to the Oriental scores.

Backman did not give test scores, rather she gave scores for six ability factors that were derived from test results by factor analysis. Thanks to Flanagan and Cooley (1966, pp. 77-81), we have an account of what these factors measure: (1) **Visual reasoning,** visualizing the outcomes of manipulating figures in two and three dimensional space, plus seeing relationships in complex nonverbal patterns; (2) **Perceptual speed and accuracy,** quick taking of information from tables, comparing names and objects to see if identical; (3) **Short-term memory,** memorizing sentences and recalling a missing word when the assertion was re-presented with that word omitted; (4) **Verbal knowledge** or **General information,** familiarity with the vocabulary, well-known facts, and basic ideas in a wide range of areas; (5) **Mathematics,** mastery of high school mathematics inclusive of algebra, geometry, analytic geometry, and calculus, also fractions and decimals; (6) **English language,** English spelling, capitalization, punctuation, and usage. Flanagan and Cooley classified the first three of these factors as aptitudes, the second three as knowledge traits.

TABLE 2.4
Project Talent: Mean Scores of Orientals, 12th Grade (N = 150)

Aptitudes			Knowledge traits		
Visual reasoning	Perceptual speed and accuracy	Short-term memory	General information	High school mathematics	English language
96.54	101.69	101.53	95.74	111.65	102.65

Aptitude average: 99.92   Knowledge average: 103.35

IQ narrow			Achievement narrow	
Nonverbal	Verbal	Overall	Mathematics	English
96.54	–	–	111.65	102.65

IQ broad			Achievement broad		
Nonverbal	Verbal	Overall	Mathematics	English	Perceptual
96.54	95.74	96.14	111.65	102.65	101.69

Example of calculations:

(1) Backman Oriental score for visual reasoning (VIS) = 49.4, White score = 51.8; (2) 49.4 – 51.8 = –2.4, that + 10 (Backman SD) = –.24 $SDU;$ (3) –.24 times 15 and divided by 14 = –.257 White $SDU;$ (4) White mean = 100, White SD = 15; (5) –.257 x 15 = – 3.86, that + 100 = 96.14; (6) 96.14 + .88 (compensation for Orientals less elite) –.48 (compensation for Whites include Hispanics) = **96.54** as Oriental mean for visual reasoning.

The first set of results in Table 2.4 follows Flanagan and Cooley: Orientals match Whites in aptitude at about 100, score above them in knowledge at about 103. But this dichotomy is not very helpful in terms of our purpose, that is, comparing IQ and achievement. Among the factors labelled aptitudes, most would not qualify as good measures of IQ and among the factors labelled knowledge traits, there is one which might well qualify, namely, general information.

The second set of results in Table 2.4 offers a dichotomy between IQ and achievement. It is based on a narrow notion of IQ as in the Coleman Report. Therefore, only visual reasoning qualifies as a measure of IQ, that is, as a measure of nonverbal IQ. Taking achievements narrowly, as school-taught subjects, only mathematics and English qualify. When we compare the results for IQ and achievement, they reveal something of great interest: Orientals overperform by 15 points on mathematical achievement, that is, they have a nonverbal IQ of 96.5 and a high school mathematics score of 111.6. This is all the more surprising because spatial ability is held to be a prerequisite for mathematical achievement. The Coleman Report (Table 2.3) found a close match between nonverbal IQ and mathematics, but recall that the latter emphasized problem solving rather than mastery of school-taught material. The Project Talent tests emphasized not only school mathematics but also advanced mathematics and, in my opinion, these two factors have reinforced one another and dug a huge gulf between IQ and achievement.

The third set of results in Table 2.4 offer a dichotomy between IQ and achievement based on the broader Wechsler notion of IQ. This means that general information and vocabulary qualify as measures of verbal IQ and now, Orientals show a 7-point gap between verbal IQ and English language achievement. We also have a full range of scores for Oriental IQ circa 1960, namely, 96 for overall IQ with nonverbal a bit higher and verbal a bit lower. Indeed, the nonverbal and verbal values differ by less than one point. This is far less than the Coleman Report difference for 12th graders of 3.62 points. The Coleman Report result must be preferred, given that Project Talent had a high nonresponse rate and their Oriental sample numbered only 150.

THE ETHNIC MINORITIES RESEARCH PROJECT

Estimate: Taken together, Chinese and Japanese public school pupils get 98 for overall IQ. Adjustments: Initial estimate lowered 3 points because of obsolete norms.

This project was conducted by the Urban Institute under the direction of Thomas Sowell. Sowell (1986, p. 63) emphasized the hazards of using the body of data collected for between-group comparisons and when I stress its limitations, this should not be taken as criticism of the Project or its director. When necessary, I have made my own tabulations from the data tapes and when doing so, have eliminated a few Chinese subjects with zero IQs. Presumably these were school children who handed in blank answer sheets or were perceived as having too little English to be tested. The best IQ data come from 1950 to 1971, the period surrounding the Coleman Report and Project Talent. Since results were collected only for ethnic minorities, Chinese and Japanese cannot be measured against Whites in general, but they can be compared to certain subgroups within the White population, namely, German, Irish, Italian, and Polish Americans.

Rather than taking random or stratified national samples, Sowell targeted schools and school districts with high concentrations of minority pupils by using a wide range of personal and institutional contacts. The samples for the four White ethnic groups total 9,725 subjects for the 1950s, 7,189 for the 1960s, 679 for 1970-1971, and come from a variety of locales (Sowell, 1978a, pp. 210 and 232-233). However, all four have a metropolitan bias, most school districts are below average in income, and parental occupation shows unskilled and semi-skilled workers outnumbering all others by a ratio of 2.5 to 1. Setting aside samples too small to be significant, Chinese subjects over these periods total 1824 and break down as follows: 56% from one private school in one Chinatown; 17% from public schools in that same Chinatown; and 27% from public schools elsewhere. Collectively they have a median income well below average and workers outnumber all other occupations by a ratio of 1.8 to 1. The only significant Japanese sample is 123 subjects from the 1950s, all from one Western town and almost all working class (Sowell & King, 1975).

Comparing the Chinese and Japanese samples to the four White ethnic groups makes sense only if: German, Irish, Italian, and Polish Americans collectively have a mean IQ equivalent to White Americans in general; the Chinese/Japanese and Whites respectively were scored on comparable tests with comparable norms. Unfortunately the group IQs were from pooled data, that is, scores from virtually all IQ tests then in common use were treated as equivalent and merged. The tapes (Sowell & King, 1975) were not of much help. They gave test names for few Chinese and no Japanese; they named the tests taken by many Whites but omitted the edition and date of publication. You cannot count on schools using the most recent test in print, rather they tend to use up backlogs of old tests and purchase obsolete tests if they can get them at a discount. This assertion may arouse skepticism but the tendency in question is amply evidenced by studies from a number of locales. Therefore, we can only hope that all groups took tests with much the same amount of obsolescence and that their scores were inflated to much the same degree.

TABLE 2.5

Ethnic Minorities Research Project

Mean IQs Chinese and Japanese Schoolchildren, Measured Against White Ethnic Groups

Dates	Groups and IQs			
	German	Irish	Italian	Polish
1950–1959	102	105	99	104
1960–1969	106	107	103	107
1970–1971	105	105	100	109
	White Average	Chinese private school	Chinese public school	Japanese public school
1950–1959	102.50	106.18	100.83	101.20
1960–1969	105.75	107.51	103.16	–
1970–1971	104.75	109.42	–	–

	Chinese private school		Chinese public school		Japanese public school	
	IQ adjusted	N	IQ adjusted	N	IQ adjusted	N
1950–1959	103.68	254	98.33	748	98.70	123
1960–1969	101.76	683	97.41	58	–	–
1970–1971	104.67	81	–	–	–	–

Table 2.5 is divided into three steps: first, the inflated IQs of the four White groups are presented; second, their average, labelled as the White average, is compared to the inflated IQs of the Chinese and Japanese samples; finally, the White average is set at 100 and the Chinese and Japanese scores adjusted downwards accordingly. The public school IQs give familiar results, with an overall mean for Chinese of 97 to 98 and essential parity between Chinese and Japanese. As for the Chinese private school, at least for the 1950s, we can compare its pupils to Chinese from public schools in general and Chinese from public schools in its own Chinatown: it is 5.35 points above the former and 2.58 points above the latter. It appears to profit from both a regional bias and positive selection within its area. Sowell speculated that it was a Catholic parochial school. Catholicism is a minority religion among Chinese Americans and perhaps parents who patronize parochial schools, and pay their fees, have higher than usual aspirations for their children's education (Sowell, 1978a, pp. 210-213; 1986, pp. 50-51).

SUMMARY

The three great national surveys gave very similar results. The Project Talent 12th graders are about two points below the 12th graders from the Coleman Report. However, the Project Talent value for overall IQ of 96.14 is only .68 points below the Coleman Report value for grades 3 to 12 and, of course, the variation from grade to grade could be sampling error. As for the Ethnic Minorities Research Project, when the values for Chinese and Japanese public school children are averaged, their mean IQ comes to 98.48. This is actually identical to the overall IQ of high school students from the Coleman Report! Given the ambiguities of sampling and scoring, this must be ascribed to Divine Providence rather than anything else. Nonetheless, however we compare them, the national surveys vary within a very narrow range of one or two IQ points.

3

Eleven Studies
from Various Locales

The Ethnic Minorities Research Project was the last national survey of Asian and White American IQ. However, since 1960, there have been 11 studies of various locales, that is, neighborhoods, school districts, cities, states, or universities. These can be classified as follows: studies whose subjects were tested in the 1960s, that is, before the huge influx of post-1968 Asian immigrants had its impact; two studies of San Francisco's Chinatown that allow us to assess the initial impact of that influx, at least on one community; recent studies of little value, either because their subjects were university students or graduates, or because they lump together all of the diverse subgroups of today's Asian American community.

KAUAI ISLAND 1965-1966

Estimates: Japanese get 99 for nonverbal IQ, 97 for verbal IQ. Adjustments: Initial estimates lowered 10 points because of obsolete norms.

Kauai is the northwesternmost island of the Hawaiian chain and in 1960 it had a population of 30,000. During 1955, there were 800 live births of which 280 were Japanese. Werner, Simonian, and Smith (1968) conducted a longitudinal study of these children and, in 1965 to 1966, gave them the

SRA Primary Mental Abilities Test, Elementary Form, 1954 edition. The Japanese children now aged 9 to 10 years numbered 253, so attrition was less than 10%. Their socioeconomic status based on father's occupation was assessed at about average, with 17% professional and managerial, 54% skilled and technical, 29% semiskilled or unskilled.

Werner et al. (1968, p. 48) put their mean IQ at 108 and, initially, this seemed a very good performance. Although the White children tested had a mean of 112, they were primarily of the professional and managerial class and numbered only 18, far too few to serve as a comparison group. However, an IQ score is only as good as the norms on which it is based and investigation revealed a surprising fact: the norms used suffered from a total of 33.5 years of obsolescence. Werner had not used the 1962 edition of the PMA test, but the 1954 edition, presumably because a backlog was available. The 1954 test manual and technical supplement tell a sad story.

The manual (Thurstone & Thurstone, 1954a, p. 1) says that the test has been "improved" by having its norms equated with those of the Stanford-Binet, which refers of course to the 1937 Stanford-Binet whose standardization sample was tested in 1932 (Flynn, 1984b, p. 30). The technical supplement (Thurstone & Thurstone, 1954b, pp. 2-4) tells why. In 1951, the Thurstones found that their test was giving lower IQs than the Stanford-Binet and adjusted their norms accordingly. Actually, assuming the PMA test was normed in 1946 (shortly before the 1948 edition), the score difference was not a product of bad sampling but of IQ gains over time. Flynn (1984b, p. 35) showed that IQ gains in America since 1932 have proceeded at a general rate of .3 points per year. The 14 years between 1932 and 1946 would mean a gain of 4.2 IQ points, and would toughen the PMA norms by that amount, which predicts almost perfectly the 4.3-point deficit that so disturbed the Thurstones (Thurstone & Thurstone, 1954b, p. 3). In 1954, rather than realizing their norms needed to be updated, they projected them even further back into the past, presenting norms that were 22 years obsolete on the day of publication. In 1965-1966, when Werner et al. scored their Japanese subjects against them, the norms were 33.5 years obsolete and inflated the IQ scores by 10.05 points (.3 points per year x 33.5 years = 10.05).

Table 3.1 first gives the inflated values for the five factors of the PMA test and for PMA overall IQ. The number subtest, which is elementary addition problems, and the space subtest, selecting the missing part of a square, are not counted when calculating a PMA IQ. Table 3.1 then attempts to break down the overall IQ into nonverbal and verbal scores. The verbal estimate is

TABLE 3.1
Kauai Island 1965 to 1966
Mean IQ of Japanese, Ages 9 to 10 years, SRA Primary Mental Abilities Test (N = 253)

Factors					
Verbal	Space	Reasoning	Perception	Number	PMA IQ
107	105	112	105	106	108

	IQ		
	Nonverbal[a]	Verbal	Overall
Norms unadjusted	109.00	107.00	108.00
Norms adjusted	98.95	96.95	97.95

[a] An estimate derived as described in text.

well-founded in that the PMA verbal score is based entirely on a vocabulary test using both words and pictures. The nonverbal estimate is based simply on the fact that the other tests collectively are mainly nonverbal and, given a verbal IQ of 107 and an overall IQ of 108, the nonverbal score should be about 109. Finally, Table 3.1 attempts to compensate for the radical obsolescence of the Stanford-Binet norms. The Binet does not differentiate between nonverbal and verbal IQ, so all scores were lowered by 10.05 points. This gives adjusted values of nonverbal IQ 98.95, verbal IQ 96.95, and overall IQ 97.95, virtually identical with our three national surveys.

At one time, I was impressed by the fact that the Japanese children scored higher on the reasoning subtest than they did overall. But that was true for every ethnic group save one (Werner et al., 1968, p. 48), so probably norms on that subtest had simply become more obsolete than the test norms as a whole.

BERKELEY, THE UNIVERSITY 1966

Estimate: Taken together, Chinese and Japanese get 94 for verbal IQ when scored against White classmates at Berkeley. Adjustments: Elite Whites, so their attenuated variance was corrected and the White mean set at 100.

In the fall of 1966, 3,053 students entered the first-year class (13th grade) of the University of California at Berkeley. They were asked to participate in a testing program that included the School and College Ability Tests

(SCAT), Form UA, and about 90% of each ethnic group did so. Sue and Kirk (1973, p. 143) gave results for American-born Chinese, American-born Japanese, and all others who were called the control group. The ethnic break-down of the control group was not given, but comparison of several sources suggests an estimate of 93% White and 7% non-White, mainly Chinese and Japanese born outside the United States, Filipinos, Blacks, and Hispanics (Jensen, 1973, p. 230; Sue & Kirk, 1972, p. 471).

When applicants from various ethnic groups meet the same academic criteria to gain entry to a particular university, this serves as an equalizer. Therefore, whatever between-group IQ differences may exist among Berkeley students cannot be assumed to correspond to those existent among the general population and usually I have included university samples only for the sake of completeness. However, since the Berkeley data assumes importance when we reach the section on IQ and achievement, it merits a full analysis.

As for the Berkeley tests, the SCAT verbal correlates with Wechsler verbal IQ at the .84 level and qualifies as a verbal IQ test. But the SCAT quantitative is **not** a nonverbal IQ test, rather it measures something closer to mathematical achievement. The correlation with Wechsler performance IQ is only .56 and correlations with school mathematics marks, even when awarded 9 months later, run from .58 to .78 except where variance is clearly attenuated (Educational Testing Service, 1962, pp. 5, 7, and 24). Also, at Berkeley within every ethnic group, men had a SCAT quantitative score 10 to 12 points (White SD = 15) above women, a difference unheard of for nonverbal IQ but typical for mathematical achievement. The test content adds further confirmation, that is, it corresponds to skills and processes schools tend to teach (Anastasi, 1968, pp. 224-225 and 400-402). The knowledge assumed is not too advanced; for example, the university version used at Berkeley has little beyond elementary Algebra. Putting the Coleman Report mathematics test at one extreme, so much problem solving as to be virtually an IQ test, and the Project Talent mathematics tests at the other extreme, advanced school-taught mathematics such as analytic geometry and calculus, the SCAT quantitative would fall in between.

Turning to the Berkeley sample, note that the American-born Chinese and Japanese entrants were not compared to Whites but to a control group which was only 93% White. Therefore, we must extract a raw score mean for Whites alone, because the 7% non-Whites would tend to be lower scoring, at least on the verbal subtests. Assuming that non-Whites scored no better than American-born Chinese, a minimal assumption, this raises the control group mean from 36.80 to 37.24 for Whites. We must also estimate an unattenuated SD for Whites, because the fact Berkeley admits only elite students would drastically restrict both score variance and the standard

TABLE 3.2
University of California, Berkeley, 1966
Mean Scores of Chinese (N = 210) and Japanese (N = 99), 13th Grade

	SCAT		
	Verbal	Quantitative	
Chinese	92.15	102.56	White means = 100.00
Japanese	94.96	102.00	

	IQ		Achievement	
	Verbal	Nonverbal	Mathematics	
				White means
Chinese	115.15	121.88	125.56	= 123.00
Japanese	117.96	125.18	125.00	

Examples of calculations:

Chinese/White verbal gap: (1) Chinese raw score mean = 30.95 and White mean = 37.24; (2) White SD = 12.025 (corrected for attenuation); (3) 30.95 – 37.24 = –6.29, that + 12.025 = –.523 SDU; (4) –.523 x 15 = –7.85 as Chinese/White gap in IQ points.

Chinese nonverbal IQ: (1) 115.15 (sample verbal mean) - 96.70 (population verbal mean) = 18.45 as verbal gap between sample and population; (2) 18.45 + 15.41 (verbal SD) = 1.197 as that gap in SDU; (3) Assuming nonverbal gap the same, 1.197 x 18.07 (nonverbal SD) = 21.63 IQ points; (4) 21.63 + 100.25 (population nonverbal mean) = **121.88** as sample nonverbal mean.

deviation. I used a multiplier of 1.30 derived from Wechsler data, for groups similarly elite (Flynn, 1984b, p. 37), which put the unattenuated White SD at 12.025 raw score points. This value makes excellent sense when compared to those in the test manual (Educational Testing Service, 1961, Table 5). The usual calculation of deviation scores, using the adjusted values, is detailed in the first example at the bottom of Table 3.2.

Table 3.2 first presents SCAT results with the mean of White entrants set at 100, which puts Chinese and Japanese at 92 and 95 respectively on the verbal subtests, both at about 102 on the quantitative subtests. In fact, as a highly selected elite, White entrants at Berkeley would have a mean far above 100. I have put it at 123, based on their SAT scores (Jensen, 1973, pp. 229 and 232) and the correlation between the SAT and IQ (Razz, Willerman, Ingmundsen, & Hanlon, 1983). This estimate is only approximate, but what is important is not the absolute value but the score differences between

Chinese, Japanese, and Whites. Putting Whites at 123, Table 3.2 gives Chinese 115 for verbal IQ (based on the SCAT verbal) and 126 for mathematical achievement (based on the SCAT quantitative); it gives Japanese 118 and 125 respectively.

What is missing are values for nonverbal IQ. Given the nature of the SCAT quantitative test, school-taught arithmetic and elementary Algebra, we would expect Chinese and Japanese to show a nonverbal IQ/mathematics gap somewhere between the nil points of the Coleman Report and the 15 points of Project Talent. Just to see whether the Berkeley data at least plausibly conforms to that pattern, I decided to estimate values for nonverbal IQ. The Coleman Report means and *SDs* for 12th graders were assumed to be valid for the general population of both Chinese and Japanese; and Berkeley entrants were assumed to be equally highly selected for both verbal and nonverbal IQ. The calculations are at the bottom of Table 3.2 and the results in Table 3.2. On the basis of these estimates, Chinese at Berkeley had a nonverbal IQ of 122 and overperformed by 4 points on SCAT mathematics, whereas Japanese at 125 merely matched their mathematics score.

BERKELEY, THE SCHOOLS 1968

Estimates: Chinese and Japanese get 98 for nonverbal IQ, 95 for verbal IQ. Adjustments: Initial estimates are from an elite area and are based on all races and obsolete norms; they drop by 18-20 points when Chinese and Japanese are scored against local Whites.

In the spring of 1968, Jensen and Inouye administered a battery including the Lorge-Thorndike Intelligence Test, 1957 edition, and the Stanford Achievement Test, 1964 edition, to children from kindergarten to grade 6 in the Berkeley, California public schools (Jensen, personal communications, July 27, 1987, August 27, 1987, and June 20, 1988). At grades 4 to 6, Orientals numbered 234 and Whites 1,506. Orientals included only Chinese and Japanese and census data indicate a ratio in favor of Chinese of two or three to one.

The Berkeley children received very high IQ scores, partially due to the fact that the Berkeley area is elite in terms of SES, partially due to obsolete norms based on a standardization sample inclusive of all races. The 1957 Lorge-Thorndike norms were based on the standardization sample of 1953 whose performance by then had been fully analyzed (Lorge & Thorndike, 1954, pp. 2-4; 1957, pp. 5-6 and 16). Therefore, the Berkeley data must be adjusted for obsolescence from 1953 to 1968 and later, when we get to Jensen's study of Chinatown schools, we will have to adjust Lorge-

Thordike scores from as late as 1975. Unfortunately, there is only one study of Lorge-Thordike obsolescence (Hieronymus & Stroud, 1969). It covered only 1953 to 1963 and revealed an eccentric pattern. For example, 7th graders at the 120 IQ level showed a nonverbal gain of 9 points and a verbal gain of only 4 points, whereas 4th graders showed a gain of 2 points for both. Clearly these results do not represent true IQ gains but problems with the norms at various ages and IQ levels. However, the overall pattern is a familiar one: taking all grades and all IQs within the normal range, those from 80 to 120, the average gain is 3.33 points over the decade for nonverbal IQ, 3.06 points for verbal.

In calculating Lorge-Thorndike obsolescence, I decided to assume that it approximates the Wechsler pattern for school children. This has the virtue of covering most of the relevant period with data from similar tests. From 1947-1948 to 1972, the Wechsler rate of gain for full scale IQ was .313 points per year (7.68 points ÷ 24.5 years); nonverbal gains were a bit higher at .354 points, verbal gains a bit lower at .273 points (Flynn, 1984a, p. 288; 1985, p. 238). There is good evidence that the Lorge-Thorndike also had differential rates for nonverbal and verbal IQ. For example, the unadjusted IQs for Whites from Berkeley 1968 (Table 3.3) show nonverbal IQ about 2 points higher than verbal; and the data for Bakersfield 1969-1970 (Table 3.8) show nonverbal IQ fully 8 points higher. The most parsimonious explanation is that when the test was normed in 1953, White nonverbal and verbal IQ were equal but later they became unequal due to differential rates of gain. As for the fact that the Lorge-Thorndike standardization sample of 1953 contained all races, no ethnic breakdown of the sample is given. In order to approximate White norms, I am allowing 2.5 points, which is the average of the difference non-Whites made in the Wechsler and Stanford-Binet standardization samples of 1972 (Flynn, 1984b, pp. 30-31).

These approximations are rough indeed, but faced with Lorge-Thorndike data whose obsolescence varies from 15 to 22 years, there are only two choices: scrap the data entirely or make rough adjustments. I decided to pursue the latter course, while emphasizing that caution would dictate the former. At any rate, we can now adjust the Berkeley IQs so as to score the subjects against nationwide norms, Whites only, circa 1968: nonverbal scores, deduct 7.81 points, 5.31 for obsolescence (.354 x 15 years) plus 2.5 points for all races; verbal scores, deduct 6.60 points, 4.10 for obsolescence (.273 x 15 years) plus 2.5.

TABLE 3.3
Berkeley Public Schools 1968
Mean Scores of Orientals (N = 234) and Whites (N = 1506), Grades 4 to 6

	IQ unadjusted			IQ adjusted (N)		
	Nonverbal	Verbal	Overall	Nonverbal	Verbal	Overall
Oriental	118.34	113.09	115.72	110.53	106.49	108.51
Whites	120.17	118.37	119.27	112.36	111.77	112.07

	IQ adjusted (L)			Achievement (L)		
	Nonverbal	Verbal	Overall	Maths	English	Overall
Oriental	98.17	94.72	96.45	98.75	98.61	98.68

Key to norms: IQ unadjusted = scored against national norms, all races, 1953; IQ adjusted (N) = scored against national norms, Whites, 1968; IQ adjusted (L) = scored against local norms, Whites, 1968; Achievement (L) = scored against local norms, Whites, 1968.

In Table 3.3, "IQ unadjusted" are the inflated scores Berkeley school children got when scored against all races norms 15 years obsolete. "IQ adjusted (N)" are what they get when scored against nationwide White norms that are current. The latter reveal the true extent to which the Berkeley area is elite: a mean IQ of 112 for White school children in that area is far more plausible than 119. The values labelled "IQ adjusted (L)" are the significant ones for our purposes. Berkeley Orientals are simply scored against Berkeley Whites with the White means set at 100, so as to strip away the elite character of the area. When this is done, Berkeley Orientals get 98 for nonverbal, 95 for verbal, and 96.45 for overall IQ, an almost perfect match for grades 3 to 12 from the Coleman Report.

The values labelled "Achievement (L)" are the result of scoring Orientals against local Whites on the Stanford Achievement Test (Vernon, 1982, p. 33). The English score shows that Orientals performed 4 points above their average verbal IQ, although half of this was superior spelling. The Mathematics score shows that Orientals did no better than match their nonverbal IQ. This is an atypical result, for the Stanford arithmetic tests emphasize primarily school-taught material rather than general problem-solving skills (Bryan, 1965, pp. 115-118 and 123; Stake & Hastings, 1965, pp. 124-125).   These subjects are, of course, elementary school children doing elementary rather than advanced mathematics. We have hypothesized that Chinese and Japanese open up an IQ/achievement gap to the extent to which mathematics is both school taught and advanced and therefore, a hypothesis that the gap will appear in high school rather than elementary school is a natural extension. But data from one school district is a slender thread on which to hang such a conjecture.

The preceding results are all for grades 4 to 6. Children at lower levels took no achievement tests but did take IQ tests. Kindergarten to grade 3 took the Lorge-Thorndike Pictorial Test and, when scored against Berkeley Whites, Orientals averaged 98.65. Kindergarten to grade 4 took the Figure Copying Test: Orientals scored 102 below grade 3, 108 at grades 3 and 4.

LOS ANGELES 1969-1970

Estimates: Chinese and Japanese get 99 for nonverbal IQ, 95 for verbal IQ. Adjustments: Local Whites assessed as unrepresentative so rough estimates obtained by norming on local Blacks.

Under Project Access, a program to provide access to post-secondary education for minority and disadvantaged students, a nine-test battery was administered in the 1969-1970 school year. The only relevant data is from Los Angeles where approximately 305 White, 390 Oriental, 2,600 Black, and 1,020 Mexican-American 11th grade students both designated their ethnicity and sat the tests. Flaughter (personal communication, August 13, 1987) has supplied the raw score means and *SDs* for all tests, allowing for the calculation of deviation scores by the usual method.

In order to obtain nonverbal IQs, the scores of three tests were averaged: letter groups in which five sets of four letters are presented, the set that does not fit to be identified; choosing a path which measures the ability to comprehend the pattern in a complex network of lines; and figure analogies which uses small geometric designs and figures. For verbal IQ, the vocabulary and reading comprehension tests were averaged. There was also a mathematics test, mathematical quantities were to be compared to determine equality or inequality, and a test of English grammar and punctuation. Two other tests were set aside as testing skills other than reasoning ability or academic achievement, namely, associative memory and ability to follow directions (Flaughter, 1971).

TABLE 3.4

Los Angeles 1969 to 1970: Comparisons of Project Access Sample with Los Angeles
(SMSA) High School Population, in Terms of Percentages of Four Ethnic Groups

| | | Project Access | |
Groups	Los Angeles	Unadjusted	Adjusted (LA)
White	71.44	7.07	71.44
Oriental	2.32	9.04	2.78
Mexican	13.37	23.64	7.26
Black	12.87	60.25	18.52

Key to adjustment: Adjusted (LA) = the Project Access sample with the percentage of
Whites increased to equal the percentage in the Los Angeles Standard Metropolitan
Statistical Area, the ratios among the other groups held constant.

The Project Access sample did not accurately represent the ethnic mix of
the Los Angeles metropolitan area (Los Angeles-Long Beach). It comprised
13 predominantly Black and Mexican American high schools whose few
White students were a residual group in the sense that they had not joined
other Whites in the move to suburban schools. Table 3.4, drawn from the
1970 census, shows that over 70% of the Los Angeles high school
population was White as compared to 7% of the sample. Orientals actually
outnumber Whites in the sample despite being only 2% of the population.
This counts as Oriental all Chinese, Japanese, and Koreans (few) and half of
Southeast Asians (very few even in 1970). Table 3.4 also adjusts the Project
Access sample to bring Whites up to their actual population percentage,
while keeping the ratios between other groups constant. The rationale is to
see whether any other group is underrepresented, which would be at least
prima facie evidence that it too was residual. The adjustment reveals that
Orientals and Blacks were both overrepresented and that Mexican Americans
were underrepresented, although this last may be a result of which schools
chose to participate rather than selective migration.

There is ample evidence that the White sample has been strongly affected
by negative selection. First, Whites and Blacks are equal for socioeconomic
status, the large SES advantage Whites normally enjoy having disappeared,
while Orientals are above both (Flaughter, 1971, p. 12). However, the
effects of negative selection go beyond that: as Jensen (1980, p. 44) pointed
out, matching Whites and Blacks for SES usually eliminates only 3 points of
the 15-point IQ gap between White and Black; here it has eliminated over 7
points. Flaughter (unpublished memorandum, September 25, 1970)
provided data that reinforce the point. For example, even the few high-SES
Whites in the sample have abnormally low educational aspirations, falling
below those of low-SES Blacks and Orientals and barely exceeding those of
low-SES Mexican Americans.

TABLE 3.5

Los Angeles 1969 to 1970

Mean IQ and Achievement Test Scores of Orientals, 11th Grade (N = 390)

	IQ			Achievement		
Group	Nonverbal	Verbal	Overall	Math	English	Overall
Normed on Whites						
Oriental	107.30	102.59	104.94	110.88	105.77	108.33
Blacks	92.31	92.76	92.53	–	–	–
Normed on Blacks						
Oriental	98.99	94.83	96.91	102.57	98.01	100.29

Key to norms: Normed on Whites = scored against White members of Project Access Sample, White means and *SDs* set at 100 and 15; Normed on Blacks = scored against Black IQ means, with Black nonverbal set at 84 and verbal at 85.

Example of calculations, Oriental nonverbal IQ normed on Blacks:

(1) 107.30 (Oriental mean normed on Whites) – 92.31 (Black mean) = 14.99; (2) 14.99 + 84.00 (set value for Black mean) = **98.99**.

In Table 3.5, initially both Orientals and Blacks are normed on the White sample in the usual way, which gives Oriental IQs of 107 nonverbal, 103 verbal, and 105 overall. These are inflated by the substandard quality of the White sample, as are the White-normed achievement test scores. However, taken together, they do reveal the usual tendency of Chinese and Japanese Americans to score higher on achievement tests than IQ. The Project Access mathematics test assumes some knowledge of high school mathematics but places considerable emphasis on novel problem solving. Therefore, it is much closer to the mathematics test of the Coleman Report than to that of Project Talent and the nonverbal IQ/mathematics achievement gap of 3.58 points falls into place between the gaps of those two studies. The verbal IQ/English achievement gap is 3.18 points, which is somewhat less than that of Project Talent but here I can see no difference between the tests. Since all White-normed values are inflated, I have provided alternative values by scoring Oriental IQ and achievement against the **Black** sample as described at the bottom of Table 3.5. The Black norms are taken from the WISC-R standardization sample of 1972 (Jensen & Reynolds, 1982, p. 425).

The alternative scores give Orientals 99 for nonverbal IQ, 95 for verbal IQ, and 97 overall. Therefore, Project Access gives no cause to reconsider estimates of Oriental IQ evidenced by better data. But even the Black-normed values rest on samples that are suspect. As inner-city residents, both Orientals and Blacks were probably negatively selected to some degree; the fact that neither group is underrepresented is weak evidence that it was to the same degree.

HAWAII 1960

Estimate: Taken together, Chinese and Japanese get 96 for verbal IQ. Adjustments: Initial estimate lowered 7.68 points because local Caucasian sample unrepresentative of local Whites; nationwide White norms would take scores lower still.

In December 1960, the Department of Education selected a random sample from all 10th grade students in public high schools in Hawaii. The principals of the 28 schools were requested to administer both the verbal and quantitative subtests of the SCAT Form 2A, 1955 edition, and the advanced Mathematics Test Form X, 1957 edition, from the California Achievement Tests (CAT) series. In April 1963, the principals were asked to administer the same tests to all 12th grade students. Over 80% of those tested in grade 10 were retested in grade 12 and Stewart, Dole, and Harris (1967) reported results for those students. They included 88 Caucasians, 64 Chinese, and 490 Japanese.

In analyzing the results, I scored Chinese and Japanese performance on the SCAT verbal against both the Hawaiian Caucasians and the White members of the nationwide SCAT standardization sample of 1955, allowing for obsolescence. Local norms gave an average verbal IQ of 103.43 and national norms 92.56. This means that the Hawaiian Caucasians were 10.78 points below the White members of the SCAT nationwide sample, a discrepancy far too great to be explained by regional variation. Clearly something was wrong with either the local or national sample. The latter appears well selected, 9352 students from 35 high schools, chosen as typical academically from a nationwide random sample and then balanced for region and size of community (Educational Testing Service, 1955, pp. 16-17).

The local sample is another matter. Assuming the Department did make a random selection from 10th graders in Hawaiian public schools, something went badly wrong either when the students were tested in the 10th grade or by the time they were retested in the 12th grade. Census data show that random selection would produce a sample 38% Japanese and 20% Caucasian. Yet results are reported for a sample 58% Japanese and 10% Caucasian, which means that half of all Caucasians had gone missing (Bureau of the Census, 1960, Hawaii, Tables 15, 46 and 101; Stewart et al., 1967, Tables 1 and 2).

Dole (personal communication, June 7, 1988) suggests that between the 10th and 12th grades, Caucasians were much more likely to leave Hawaii or transfer to private schools while Japanese were likely to remain. This could explain the underrepresentation of Caucasians but not the overrepresentation of Japanese. Simple arithmetic shows that given an initial sample 38% Japanese, and given that four-fifths of the 10th graders tested were retested in the 12th grade, the percentage of Japanese could not rise above 48% (.38 + .80 = .48). This is well short of the 58% to be explained. Therefore, I suggested that only 16 of the 28 high schools participated, my concern being less that Japanese were overrepresented in those schools than that Caucasians were so much underrepresented. However, Dole (personal communication, October 5, 1988) talked to Harris whose recollection was that all schools participated. It is logically possible that within each school, the list of students to be tested had few Japanese absentees but many from all other ethnic groups, but this seems too odd to be true.

Until the loss of half the Caucasian subjects is explained, the possibility of a residual and substandard Caucasian sample is open. As for the total sample, setting aside its racial imbalance, there is an ambiguity about its total size. The published version referred to a 20% random selection from all public school 10th graders, unpublished material speaks of 13% (Dole, personal communication, July 7, 1988), and the actual results sample comprised only 8%. If total attrition was less than the published version suggested, it becomes even more difficult to explain the racial imbalance through any of the three forms of attrition suggested. The unpublished material also gives SCAT results for a sample of 474 California Whites whose scores virtually match the SCAT White norms and again, reveal the Hawaiian Caucasian sample to have been substandard by over 10 IQ points. Stewart (personal communications, November 16, 1988 and December 5, 1988) said that these California Whites came from areas such as one surrounding an Air Force Base on the Northern edge of San Francisco, residential areas that seemed fairly typical. But he added that they were merely subjects for whom results happened to be at hand and that some scores may have been SCAT equivalents based on conversion tables.

Finally, note that the 1960 Hawaiian Caucasian sample is Caucasian rather than White. This renders the data noncomparable to both earlier Hawaiian studies and other studies in general. In 1938, Smith divided the Caucasian schoolchildren of Honolulu into Whites, Puerto Ricans, and Portuguese. The Portuguese came to Hawaii from the Azores and the Madeira Islands between 1878 and 1887 (Werner et al., 1968, p. 43). They have played a role analogous to Hispanics on the mainland, a Caucasian group partially alienated from mainstream White society with lower IQ and educational attainment. In Smith's public school sample, the Caucasian group breaks down into 50% White, 37% Portuguese, and 13% Puerto Rican. The minority groups are overrepresented in the public schools because 45% of Caucasians were in private schools and these were almost all mainstream Whites. The census stopped classifying Portuguese separately in 1940 but based simply on natural increase, I estimate that in 1960, Caucasians were 76% White, 18% Portuguese, and 6% Puerto Rican. Since 29% of Caucasians were still in private high schools, the values for the public school population would be about 70% White, 22% Portuguese, and 8% Puerto Rican.

In 1938, setting the White mean at 100, Portuguese verbal IQ was about 80 and Puerto Rican about 70 (Smith, 1942, pp. 55-56). However, by 1960, both groups had gained on Whites. For example, Werner et al. (1968, p. 48) got 95 on the verbal subtest of the PMA for 46 Portuguese subjects and, adjusted for obsolescence, this would be 85 (see Table 3.1); and Coleman Report data for 12th graders showed that Puerto Ricans had also attained a verbal IQ of 85 (Coleman et al., 1966b, p. 17). Therefore, if both groups were 30% of the Caucasians in public high schools, Caucasian mean IQ would have been about 95.5 or 4.5 points below the White mean.

However, 4.5 points would be the sample deficit only if the Caucasian sample was well selected. If it was indeed residual, all three Caucasian groups may have been substandard, or Portuguese and Puerto Ricans may have constituted an even larger percentage, or both. Because these possible biases cannot be measured, I have chosen to do the following: treat 4.50 points as a minimum estimate of sample deficit; treat 10.87 points, the figure suggested by the SCAT standardization sample, as a maximum estimate; and split the difference. This gives 7.68 points as the verbal IQ deficit of Stewart et al.'s Caucasian sample when compared to a representative sample of Hawaiian Whites.

Table 3.6 first gives Chinese and Japanese results based on an assumption which must be false to some degree: that Stewart et al.'s Caucasian sample was representative not only of Caucasians but also of Whites. As usual, the "White" mean has been set at 100 and deviation scores calculated on the basis of raw score means and *SDs*. Stewart et al. (1967, pp. 22-23) gave means but no *SDs*, so values for the latter were taken from the SCAT and CAT standardization samples (Educational Testing Service, 1955, Table 6; Tiegs & Clark, 1963, Table 1). Table 3.6 then gives scores based on the assumption that the Caucasian sample was unrepresentative, that is, the Caucasian mean has been set at 92.32 or at 7.68 points below the true White mean. For reasons stated, the SCAT verbal has been equated with verbal IQ and the SCAT quantitative with mathematical achievement. The CAT mathematics test is very like the SCAT quantitative with perhaps even less problem solving and a bit more school-taught calculations and information (Burch, 1953, p. 512; Findley, 1953, p. 6; North, 1959, p. 592; Schindler, 1953, p. 7).

The Table 3.6 results listed under "Verbal IQ" are our best estimates for Chinese and Japanese high school students in Hawaii in the 1960s. Scored against local White norms, their verbal IQs range from 94 to 97 and give 96 as an average. If scored against national White norms, that is, the White members of the SCAT standardization sample, they would get 3 or 4 points lower.

The size of the gap between IQ and achievement for these Chinese and Japanese subjects also depends on whether they are normed against Hawaiian Whites or US Whites. The verbal IQ/mathematics gap averages at 6.9 points on local norms, 12.7 points on national norms. If the Coleman Report is correct, nonverbal IQ would be 3.55 points higher than verbal, so the nonverbal IQ/mathematics gap would be somewhere between 3.4 points and 9.1 points.

THE CHINESE IN TRANSITION: 1972-1975

The US Immigration Act of 1965 took effect in 1968 and brought a flood of immigrants from a variety of Asian countries. It had limited impact on Japanese Americans but by 1972, new arrivals were at least 25% of Chinese Americans and sometime after 1975, they became a clear majority (Gardner et al., 1985, pp. 7-9). Unfortunately, there are only two IQ studies from this period and both are of Chinese children attending a few private schools located in San Francisco's Chinatown.

TABLE 3.6
Hawaii: Mean Scores of Chinese (N = 64) and Japanese (N = 490)
High School Students—Tested Both in 1960 and 1963

Group	Grade	SCAT		CAT	
		Verbal	Quantitative	Mathematics	
Chinese	10	102.48	108.80	111.22	
	12	104.70	109.18	109.06	Caucasian
Japanese	10	101.89	109.87	112.47	Mean = 100
	12	104.63	110.94	111.16	

Group	Grade	Verbal IQ	Math achievement		
		SCAT	SCAT	CAT	
Chinese	10	94.80	101.12	103.54	
	12	97.02	101.50	101.38	Caucasian
Japanese	10	94.21	102.19	104.79	Mean = 92.32
	12	96.95	103.26	103.48	

Group	Grade	Verbal IQ	Math achievement	
		SCAT	SCAT	
Chinese	10	91.19	103.75	
	12	94.28	105.23	SCAT White
Japanese	10	90.56	104.90	mean = 100
	12	94.20	107.11	

Calculation of scores against the White members of SCAT standardization sample.

Grade 12, Chinese verbal IQ: (1) Educational Testing Service, 1955, Table 6 gives raw score means and *SDs* for SCAT all races sample; (2) Deviation IQ against these all races norms is 99.35; (3) From Flynn (1984b, Table 1), assume a White mean of 102.45 (average of Stanford-Binet and Wechsler) and *SD* of 14 when Whites are normed against all races with mean set at 100 and *SD* at 15; (4) 99.35 – 102.45 = –3.10, as IQ points below White mean; (5) –3.10 times 15/14 equals –3.32, as IQ points below White mean with White *SD* set at 15; (6) 100 – 3.32 = 96.68 as IQ with White mean set at 100; (7) Assume 2.40 points obsolescence from 1955 to 1963 (Flynn, 1984b, p. 35); (8) 96.68 – 2.40 = **94.28** as Chinese verbal IQ against current White norms.

Grade 10. Note that here the raw score means and *SDs* for the SCAT sample can only be approximated. Educational Testing Service, 1955, pp. 38–39 suggests 29.7 as verbal raw score mean and 25.8 as quantitative. Raw score *SD* assumed to be 11.5 and 9.8 respectively (same as Grade 12), although probably a bit less.

SAN FRANCISCO 1972

Estimates: Chinese get 101 for performance IQ, 91 for verbal IQ.
Adjustments: Initial estimates lowered 8-10 points because of obsolete
norms.

Late in 1971, parents in San Francisco's Chinatown faced the prospect
that their children, who had attended local public schools in which over 90%
of pupils were Chinese, might be transported to schools in which Chinese
were a small minority. Therefore, they established several private schools
which came to be called Freedom Schools. Soon after this, in 1972 or 1973,
Yee and La Forge (1974) administered the Wechsler Intelligence Scale for
Children (WISC) to the 4th grade of one of these schools, average age 9.5
years. From the total roll of 84, they selected 53 children who were
American born and whose understanding of English was considered
adequate for their age. The examiners were all Chinese but the tests were
given in English.

Table 3.7 first presents WISC IQs for the Freedom School 4th graders.
However, the WISC standardization sample was tested in 1947-1948 and
included a quota of institutionalized mentally retarded children. Since these
Chinese children were tested circa 1972, their IQs have been inflated by 24.5
years of obsolescence and a slightly substandard sample. The appropriate
comparison group are the White members of the 1972 all races sample used
to norm the Wechsler Intelligence Scale for Children - Revised (WISC-R).
Therefore, the WISC scores have been translated into scores based on those
norms and labelled WISC-R(W) IQs. This translation is based on 33
samples totalling 1607 subjects who took both tests: it entails subtracting
8.54 points from the WISC full scale score, a point more from the
performance score, approximately a point less from the verbal score (Flynn,
1984a, p. 283; 1985, Table 1).

As Table 3.7 shows, when the Freedom School 4th graders are thus
scored against current White norms, they get 101 for performance IQ, 91 for
verbal IQ, and 96 for full scale. The value for verbal IQ is surprisingly low.
It cannot be due to post-1968 immigrants because, as described previously,
all foreign-born children were excluded from testing. The next study yields
an even lower verbal IQ in the same locale and therefore, discussion is best
left for then.

TABLE 3.7
San Francisco, Chinatown Freedom Schools, 1972
Mean IQ of Chinese, 4th Grade (N = 53)

Norms	IQ		
	Performance	Verbal	Full scale
WISC	110.70	98.60	104.80
WISC-R(W)[a]	101.16	91.06	96.26

[a] WISC-R(W) is the result of translating WISC IQs into IQs scored against the **White** members of the WISC-R standardization sample, with White mean and *SD* set at 100 and 15 respectively.

SAN FRANCISCO 1975

Estimates: Chinese get 101 for nonverbal IQ, 89 for verbal IQ. Adjustments: Initial estimates lowered by 6-10 points to compensate for all races and obsolete norms.

In the Winter of 1975, Jensen administered a battery of tests to all children from kindergarten through the 6th grade in three Freedom Schools. The tests included the Lorge-Thorndike Intelligence Tests, 1957 edition, and Raven's Coloured Matrices.   They were tested by their own teachers, who had been trained for that purpose, and above kindergarten, all test instructions were given in English. Fifty percent of the children were foreign born, their parents coming mainly from Hong Kong. Vernon (1982, pp. 23-26 and 31-32) published some of the results and Jensen (circa 1970; personal communications, July 28, 1987, August 27, 1987, and June 20, 1988) supplied other results and much helpful detail. For example, in order to assess the Freedom School results, Jensen chose White children from the public schools of Bakersfield, California as a comparison group. In fall 1969 to spring 1970, the Bakersfield children had been given the same battery of tests and, taking their scores at face value, their overall IQ was a reasonable match for the Lorge-Thorndike nationwide norms.

Focusing on Jensen's older subjects, children in grades 4 to 6, let us assume, for the moment, that his comparison group was representative of American Whites at that time. Setting the Bakersfield mean at 100, the Freedom school children would get 104 as their Lorge-Thorndike nonverbal

IQ and 98 as their verbal IQ. However, the Chinese children were tested in 1975, or 5.5 years after the Bakersfield Whites, so they would have the advantage of IQ gains over that time and their scores would have to be adjusted accordingly. Using the Wechsler nonverbal (.354 points per year) and verbal (.273 points per year) rates, that means deducting about 2 and 1.5 points respectively, putting Chinese nonverbal IQ at 102 and verbal IQ at 96.5. These values would be perfectly acceptable in the sense of being compatible with other studies. If the true means for Chinese American are 100 and 97 respectively, various samples and locales would vary by a few points.

These values may seem acceptable but, unfortunately, the assumption on which they are based is almost certainly false. After all, the fact that Bakersfield Whites in 1969-1970 matched the Lorge-Thorndike all races norms of 1953 is **not** evidence for their right to be considered representative; rather it is powerful evidence against. Actually, the performance of the Bakersfield Whites is most peculiar. When their nonverbal IQ is adjusted for 16.5 years of obsolescence (see the rates above) and all races norms (deduct another 2.5 points), it falls from 107 to 99 which makes them substandard by only one point. When their verbal IQ is adjusted, it falls from 99 to 92 making them substandard by fully 8 points. If we allow for the substandard quality of the Bakersfield Whites with whom they are compared, Chinese nonverbal IQ goes down to 101 and verbal IQ down to 88.6. Given the eccentricity of the White comparison group and how difficult it is to know what Lorge-Thorndike obsolescence was over so long a period, I would place little credibility in these estimates were it not for one thing: these Chinatown 1975 results make perfect sense in the light of the Chinatown 1972 results we derived in the last study! More on this in a moment.

Table 3.8 spells out our analysis of the 1975 Chinatown scores. First, it gives the inflated Lorge-Thorndike IQs of Bakersfield Whites, then adjusts them downward to approximate scoring against the current White norms of their time, showing the extent to which they were substandard. Second, it gives the inflated Lorge-Thorndike IQs of the Chinatown Freedom Schools, then adjusts them downward, scoring them against both Bakersfield Whites and an approximation of White norms circa 1975. Finally, it takes the Chinatown results on Raven's Coloured Matrices, converts them to deviation IQs, and makes all of the adjustments described. As the bottom of Table 3.8 shows, adjusting the Raven's results for the fact that Bakersfield Whites were substandard is complex. When you use overall IQ to measure the Bakersfield deficit, Chinatown children get a Raven's IQ of 99; when you use nonverbal IQ, they get 103. Raven's correlates about equally with both overall and nonverbal IQ.

TABLE 3.8

San Francisco, Chinatown Freedom Schools, 1975 and Bakersfield, Whites in Public
Schools, 1969–1970: Mean IQ on Various Tests, Grades 4 to 6

Lorge Thorndike

Group		IQ		
		Nonverbal	Verbal	Overall
Whites	Unadjusted[a]	107.13	99.09	103.11
(N = 698)	Adjusted[b]	98.79	92.09	95.44
Chinese	Unadjusted[a]	111.14	97.10	104.12
(N = 254)	Adjusted[c]	104.01	98.01	101.01
	Adjusted[d]	102.06	96.51	99.29
	Adjusted[e]	100.85	88.60	94.73

Raven's Coloured Matrices

Group	Median age	IQ	
		Adjusted[c]	Adjusted[e]
Chinese	9.83 years (N = 85)	105.79	99.28/102.63
	10.75 years (N = 80)	106.10	99.59/102.94

Key to norms: [a]Lorge-Thorndike, all races, 1953; [b]Lorge-Thorndike, Whites, 1969-1970; [c]Bakersfield, Whites, 1969-1970; [d]Bakersfield, Whites, 1975; [e]Lorge-Thorndike, Whites, 1975.

Example of calculations, Raven's IQ, Chinese 9.83 years of age:

To get deviation IQ: (1) Mean for Chinese that age = 29.89 (Vernon, 1982, p. 24); (2) Mean for Bakersfield Whites that age = 27.46; (3) Value for *SD* = 6.30, taking account of ceiling effect that attenuates variance for groups with mean above 25 (Jensen, 1980, p. 646); (4) 29.89 – 27.46 = 2.43, that ÷ 6.30 = .386 *SDU;* (5) .386 x 15 = 5.79, that + 100 = **105.79** as deviation IQ.

To adjust: (1) Deduct for obsolescence 1.95 points, that is, .354 points per year x 5.5 years = 1.95; (2) Deduct for Bakersfield substandard, either 4.56 points (100 – 95.44 = 4.56) using overall IQ, or 1.21 points (100 – 98.79 = 1.21) using nonverbal IQ; (3) 105.79 – 1.95 = 103.84; (4) 103.84 minus either 4.56 or 1.21 = either **99.28** or **102.63** as adjusted IQ.

As for other tests in the Chinatown battery, Chinese children aged between 5 and 10 years did far better on the Figure Copying Test than on other tests. They scored about 10 points above current White norms, plus or minus a bit depending on the degree to which Bakersfield Whites were substandard. On achievement tests, Chinese children of all ages did poorly, something to be expected on language tests given so many recent immigrants, but they also showed a marked decline on arithmetic between grades 1 and 6. Chinese parents may have paid a heavy price for switching their children to the Freedom Schools.

Let us compare our 1975 Chinatown results with our 1972 Chinatown results. In 1972, the Freedom School children got a Wechsler nonverbal IQ of 101 and verbal IQ of 91. In 1975, they got a Lorge-Thorndike nonverbal IQ of 101 and verbal IQ of 88.6. This is exactly the pattern we would expect, going from children all of whom were American born to children 50% of whom were recent arrivals. Jensen's data show that the immigrants had a differential effect: foreign birth has a mild positive correlation with Lorge-Thorndike nonverbal IQ and a negative correlation with Lorge-Thorndike verbal IQ (Vernon, 1982, p. 32). Therefore, it makes sense that nonverbal IQ would remain constant and verbal IQ would drop.

In sum, the 1972 and 1975 studies suggest that Chinese verbal IQ fell below 90 during that period in San Francisco's Chinatown. However, it would be wrong to assume that it fell that low elsewhere. The American born children from the Freedom Schools would probably be representative of the Chinatown of the mid-1960s and therefore, their results can be fairly compared with those from the Coleman Report. Comparison with the 3rd graders gives San Francisco's Chinatown a 3-point verbal deficit compared to Chinese nationwide, comparison with grades 3 to 12 a 4-point deficit; they may have had an even greater deficit compared to Chinese from the Far West (Mayeske, Okada, Cohen, Beaton, & Wisler, 1973, p. 169). The most judicious conclusion about the effects of the post-1968 immigration is this: Chinese verbal IQ nationwide probably fell a few points in the 1970s, but it may have risen since and various locales would show different values and different trends.

THE NEW ASIANS: 1976-1985

The new immigration laws eventually transformed the old Asian American community of the 1960s. By 1978, both Chinese and Filipinos outnumbered Japanese and new groups had come into prominence. Particularly after the fall of Saigon, there was a flood of refugees from Southeast Asia, and America became home to large numbers of Vietnamese, Koreans, Asian Indians, Laotians, Kampucheans, and Thais, in that order. By 1980, only 44% of the new Asian American community were Chinese or Japanese and by 1985, only 36% (Gardner et al., 1985, pp. 5-10). Moreover, thanks to a new sensitivity about studying and comparing ethnic groups, scholars dropped the term "Oriental" in favor of "Asian" and stopped identifying the locale of their studies. This meant that, aside from small samples of university students, it became impossible to isolate results for Chinese and Japanese Americans and to estimate local or regional bias.

A WESTERN CITY 1977

Estimates: Chinese and Japanese job applicants get 99 for nonverbal IQ, 92 for verbal IQ, when scored against White job applicants from the same locale. Adjustments: Elite Whites, so their attenuated variance was corrected and the White mean set at 100.

During the 1970s, the U.S. Civil Service Commission administered an examination for entry-level positions in professional and administrative occupations in the federal service. Over 80% of applicants were recent college graduates or college students within a year of their degree and the average age was always 25 years or less. Only U.S. citizens were eligible to be examined (Office of Personnel Management, U.S. Department of State, personal communication, June 1, 1988).

Wing (1980, p. 292) secured results for all those tested during one month of 1977 within the metropolitan area of a large western city. Of 1,373 applicants tested, answer sheets were found for 1,348 and 78% of these designated their racial or ethnic group. These included 710 Whites excluding Hispanics, 98 Asians excluding Filipinos, 46 Filipinos, and 91 Blacks. The Asians excluding Filipinos would have been at least 90% Chinese and Japanese and of these, few Japanese and less than 20% of Chinese would have been recent immigrants. By 1977, there were a huge number of post-1968 Asian immigrants but it takes about 6 years to become a citizen and most recent immigrants were therefore ineligible.

The examination included a mental test battery in five parts. The Verbal and Judgment tests had vocabulary, comprehension, and inference items and I have averaged their results as a measure of verbal IQ. The Induction and Number tests had letter series, figure classification, and arithmetic reasoning items and I have averaged them as a measure of nonverbal IQ. The Number test assessed general reasoning ability rather than achievement in that the quantitative skills required were held at an eighth-grade level, a level that could be assumed for most college graduates. The fifth test was Deduction, a mix of tabular and inference items, and I did not classify it as verbal or nonverbal but included it to calculate overall IQ. This means that overall IQ differs from the average of the verbal and nonverbal scores, although the differences are trivial.

TABLE 3.9

A Western City, Applicants for Professional and Administrative Posts
in the Federal Service, 1977: Mean IQ of Various Groups

Group		IQ		
		Unadjusted[a]	Adjusted[b]	Adjusted[c]
White (N = 710)	Nonverbal	105.26	–	–
	Verbal	107.15	–	–
	Overall	106.41	–	–
Asian excluding	Nonverbal	104.18	98.92	99.19
Filipino (N = 98)	Verbal	97.11	89.96	92.47
	Overall	101.08	94.67	96.00
Filipino (N = 46)	Nonverbal	87.67	82.41	86.81
	Verbal	77.26	70.11	77.58
	Overall	82.79	76.38	82.28
Black (N = 91)	Nonverbal	85.90	80.64	85.48
	Verbal	85.86	78.71	84.03
	Overall	85.70	79.29	84.47

Key to norms: [a]Nationwide population of applicants, all races; [b]Local Whites with White mean set at 100; [c]Local Whites with White SD corrected for attenuation as described in text.

Example of calculations, unadjusted nonverbal IQ, Whites:

(1) From Wing, Whites average at .3275 SDs above nationwide population on Induction and Number tests; (2) To convert from all races to White SD, .3275 x 15/14 x 15 = 5.26 IQ points for a mean of **105.26**.

Example of calculations, nonverbal IQs, Asian excluding Filipino:

(1) Unadjusted nonverbal IQ, calculated as for Whites, equals **104.18**; (2) 104.18 – 5.26 = **98.92** as adjusted nonverbal IQ scored against local White norms; (3) 100 – 98.92 = 1.08 as Asian IQ deficit inflated by attenuated variance; (4) 1.08 x .75 = 0.81 as Asian IQ deficit corrected; (5) 100 – 0.81 = **99.19** as adjusted nonverbal IQ corrected for attenuation.

Wing (1980, p. 295) presented standard scores for the ethnic groups in her sample based on the nationwide population of applicants tested at the same time. These are easily converted into deviation IQs, allowing as usual for the fact that an all races SD bears a ratio to a White SD of 15 to 14. In Table 3.9, these are labelled "unadjusted" IQs and the Whites in Wing's sample get an overall score of 106.41. The extra 6.41 points derive equally from the fact they are being scored against all races norms and from a positive regional bias. To score the other ethnic groups against Whites from their own locale, the extra points (above 100) are deducted from their unadjusted scores, which gives the first set of adjusted scores. However, these scores exaggerate the degree to which other groups fall below local Whites. The normative population is clearly elite, mainly college graduates, and the Whites therein would have an *SD* only about 75% of the general population *SD*, say 11.25 points rather than 15 points. To correct for this, the IQ deficit of each non-White group has been reduced by being multiplied by .75 and this gives the second set of adjusted scores. The calculations are spelled out at the bottom of the table.

The best estimates from Table 3.9 give Asian excluding Filipino, essentially Chinese and Japanese, 99 for nonverbal IQ, 92 to 93 for verbal IQ, and 96 for overall IQ. The values for Blacks are very close to what we know to be the mean IQ of Black Americans in general, which gives some credibility to the other estimates. The fact that most of the sample had or were getting university degrees does not seem to have acted as a leveller, does not seem to have diminished the group IQ differences normally found in the general population. This is probably because the subjects attended a wide range of universities whose admission standards varied greatly.

Aside from its elite character, the sample suffers from a range of possible biases. Whites are underrepresented compared to Asians and might be more highly selected, although only if these posts attract an elite group of college graduates which seems unlikely. Asians applied disproportionately for the higher professional posts such as accountant and engineer which may have introduced some positive selection. Although the estimates for the various ethnic groups make sense, this must be mainly fortuitous and can owe little to sample quality.

PSYCHOLOGY CLASSES 1975-1979

Estimates: Chinese and Japanese get 101 for nonverbal IQ, 98 for verbal IQ, when scored against their White classmates in psychology classes. Adjustments: Elite Whites, so their attenuated variance was corrected and the White mean set at 100.

In 1975 or 1976, Longstreth (1978) tested students from the introductory psychology course at the University of Southern California. He administered two subtests from the Cognitive Abilities Test, Nonverbal Battery, Level H to 42 Chinese and Japanese subjects and 85 Whites. This test was published in 1974 as a successor to the Lorge-Thorndike nonverbal test and the subtests used ask subjects to classify geometrical designs and fit pieces to larger forms. The Japanese would have been mainly American born but as many as half of the Chinese could have been post-1968 immigrants. Longstreth (1978, p. 292) presented results in terms of standard scores based on the multi-racial group that took introductory psychology. Therefore, translation into deviation IQs requires only the usual adjustments for the difference between all races and White *SDs* and for the attenuated *SD* of such an elite group.

In 1978 or 1979, Marsella and Golden (1980) tested undergraduate psychology classes at the University of Hawaii. They administered 20 factor-pure tests from the Kit of Reference Tests for Cognitive Factors, 1969 edition, to 118 Japanese and 101 Whites, median age 20 years. These tests measure factors ranging from verbal comprehension, word fluency, and syllogistic reasoning on the one hand, to visualization, length estimation, and number facility on the other. Using the authors' comments as a key, I have classified the tests into 11 verbal and 9 nonverbal, but the division is very rough. The Japanese subjects were Sansei or third generation Americans and had been raised in Hawaii; unfortunately, the Whites were not local but almost entirely from the mainland. As for scoring, I calculated deviation IQs for each test, then averaged these to get nonverbal, verbal, and overall IQs. The IQ gaps between Japanese and Whites would be inflated by attenuated *SDs* but deflated by averaging results from tests not perfectly correlated. Because these biases would tend to cancel out, and because the gaps are small in any event, no adjustments were attempted.

Table 3.10 shows that Chinese and Japanese psychology students at two universities had about the same mean IQ as White students, perhaps 101 to 102 nonverbal, 98 verbal, and 99 overall. These values have no general significance and these two studies have been analyzed merely for the sake of completeness. Subjects of this sort, all of whom meet the selection criteria for a particular university and for the same courses within that university, will not reflect group IQ differences found in the general population. For example, within the University of Southern California psychology course, the usual Black/White IQ gap was reduced by over 40%. This may seem at odds with the fact that when we analyzed federal job applicants, most of whom were university graduates, group IQ differences were still largely intact. But remember, a particular department at a particular university will always level differences much more effectively than a variety of universities, with a variety of standards, acting collectively.

TABLE 3.10

Psychology Classes 1975–1979: Mean IQs of Chinese and Japanese University Students, Normed Against Their White Fellow Students

			IQ		
Group	N	University	Nonverbal	Verbal	Overall
Chinese & Japanese	42	Southern California	102.01	–	–
Japanese	118	Hawaii	100.69	98.19	99.32

Calculations, University of Southern California:

(1) Standard score gap between Asians and Whites = .167 *SDs;* (2) Allowing for 15/14 ratio between all races and White *SDs*, .167 x 15/14 = .179 *SDs;* (3) Allowing for attenuated variance, .179 x .75 = .134 *SDs;* (4) Setting White mean and *SD* at 100 and 15 respectively, .134 x 15 = 2.01, that + 100 = **102.01** as nonverbal IQ.

WESTOWN 1985

Estimates: Asians get 94 for nonverbal IQ, 87 for verbal IQ. Adjustments: None because scored against a contemporary and representative sample of local Whites.

Westown is a West-Central city of substantial size with a median income close to the national average. Only 15% of its school population attend private schools and the public high school population is approximately 40% White, 30% Hispanic, 25% Black, and 5% Asian.

Circa 1985, an unnamed scholar stratified all students from grades 7 to 12 by grade and ethnic group. Within each grade/ethnic group, samples of equal size were randomly selected. In 1986 Raven reported results by age from 12.5 years to 16.5 years on both Raven's Progressive Matrices and the Mill Hill Vocabulary Scale. About 435 Whites completed both tests but Asians encountered difficulties: only 242 completed the Mill Hill, because of language problems, and only 391 completed Raven's, for reasons unstated. Assuming that equal numbers of Whites and Asians were tested, it appears that only 56% of Asians were confident in English. Two sets of results were reported for the Mill Hill based on two versions of the test. Raven asserted that the second distorts scores for both the most and least able and therefore, I analyze only the first (Raven, 1986, pp. 8, 19, 24-27, 55-58, and 77-79; personal communications, July 25, 1987 and circa August 27, 1987).

Raven reported results in terms of seven raw score cutting lines ranging from the 5th to the 95th percentiles which divide the distribution into eight segments. In order to derive raw score means and *SDs,* I used a three-step procedure based on finding the best-fitting curve: (1) Posited normalcy within each of the eight segments in terms of its distance from the overall median - which does not of course impose normalcy on the total distribution; (2) Divided the resulting curve into 20 equal segments and calculated a raw score mean for each; (3) The average of these gives the overall raw score mean and this number of evenly distributed scores affords a close estimate of the raw score *SD*.   Once these values were derived, our usual method automatically gives deviation IQs, that is, the difference between the White and Asian raw score means can be divided by the White raw score *SD* .

Table 3.11 shows that Asian adolescents in Westown in 1985 had 94 as nonverbal IQ, 87 as verbal IQ, and between 90 and 91 as overall IQ. Those under 15 years of age did about 2 points better on the matrices than the older students, but about 2 points worse on the vocabulary, resulting in similar overall IQs. If the Westown results are at all typical of the new Asian American community, that community compares unfavorably with pre-1968 Asian Americans and even with the Chinatown children of 1975, half of whom were post-1968 immigrants. The Westown verbal IQ may not appear too unfavorable, as it is only 1.5 points below Chinatown 1975, but this is deceptive. The Chinatown results included all children whereas only the top 56% of Westown Asians, those most confident in English, completed the verbal test.

Since the identity of Westown has been withheld, the best we can do to get a breakdown of the Asian sample is to focus on large central-city school districts in the West-Central region. As few as 12% of the sample may have been Chinese and Japanese, as many as 60% from Indochina. The rest were probably composed of Koreans, Filipinos, Thais, Asian Indians, and depending on how the school district classified its students, sizable groups of Iranians, Israelis, and Lebanese. Most of the Indochinese in America are refugees admitted since the fall of Saigon and at least 60% are from the second wave of refugees, boat people from Vietnam, Laos, and Kampuchea. The second wave of refugees came lacking English, possessions, and qualifications for urban occupations (Gardner et al., 1985, pp. 5, 9, and 35) and therefore, something like 36% of Westown Asians may have been disadvantaged.

The fact that Westown Asians had an overall IQ of 90 to 91, and might have had an even lower IQ if all subjects had been tested, may seem grounds for pessimism. On the other hand, their verbal scores will rise with acculturation and their nonverbal scores are encouraging when fully analysed. First, their nonverbal IQ is already somewhat higher at 94; second, when the fact they had lower SES is taken into account, Westown Asians matched Whites on the matrices test (Raven, 1986, pp. 26-27); and third, as later chapters show, Asians need not match Whites for IQ in order to match them academically.

TABLE 3.11
Westown 1985: Mean IQ of Asians, Based on Raw Scores from Raven's Progressive
Matrices and the Mill Hill Vocabulary Scale

Group	Age (years)	N	Test	Raw Scores Mean	SD
White	12·5–14·5	254	Matrices	42.92	7.03
		254	Vocabulary	34.74	8.52
	15.0–16·5	181	Matrices	48.24	6.46
		182	Vocabulary	40.00	8.41
Asian	12·5–14·5	216	Matrices	40.59	10.28
		144	Vocabulary	26.96	8.60
	15.0–16·5	175	Matrices	44.66	8.81
		98	Vocabulary	33.27	10.87

Group	Age (years)	IQ Nonverbal	Verbal	Overall
Asian	12·5–14·5	95.03	86.30	90.67
	15.0–16·5	92.69	88.00	90.35
	12·5–16·5	93.99	87.06	90.52

These speculations about the future of Asian Americans are frustrating
because different Asian groups face such different futures.   No one would
want to speculate about the future of "non-Asian" Americans without
differential data for Whites and Blacks and Puerto Ricans and Mexican
Americans. In other words, given the extraordinary diversity of the new
Asian American community, what purpose can global IQ data serve?
Certainly, such data cannot provide ethnic norms: scoring Filipinos or boat
people against Chinese or Japanese is no better than scoring Black against
White. The new Asian community might take on some social significance if
intense anti-Asian bias forced its diverse groups to coalesce and erased their
differences, but that hardly seems probable. Unless scholars break the
current taboos, and collect IQ data for Chinese, and Japanese, and Filipinos,
and Vietnamese, and so forth, the usefulness of studies of Asian American
IQ is probably at an end.

SUMMARY

Local studies tell the same story as the three great national surveys. Between 1960 and 1975, Chinese and Japanese grade and high school children had a mean IQ slightly below that of their White counterparts. Children in the Freedom Schools of San Francisco's Chinatown were a qualified exception. Although their overall IQ was well below White norms, they had a nonverbal IQ of 101. However, three other locales reported lower nonverbal scores ranging from 98 to 99. The fact that Chinese and Japanese Americans of this generation did not excel on IQ tests makes their later achievements as adults all the more remarkable. It is time to give our analysis an extra dimension. Ideally, we would discover some method of quantifying the gap between Sino-Japanese IQ and Sino-Japanese achievement.

4

Measuring the Gap
Between IQ and Achievement

Those accustomed to the assumption that group IQ and group achievement go together may need some advance evidence that Chinese and Japanese Americans really do outachieve White Americans. To anticipate, Chinese and Japanese American children born between 1945 and 1949 outperformed Whites at school. Only half as many lagged a grade or more behind their age group, 95% eventually graduated from high school as compared to under 89% of Whites. At least 50% of them took the Scholastic Aptitude Test, as compared to less than 30% of Whites, and despite this they matched White performance. They maintained the same 5 to 3 ratio when undertaking graduate study. In their early 30s, the Chinese American cohorts out-numbered Whites in high status occupations by 55% to 34%, the Japanese cohorts outnumbered Whites by 46% to 34%.

This extraordinary record of achievement will be detailed but first, we must undertake a task of measurement. Marvelling over Chinese and Japanese achievement leads nowhere except to escalating emotion. The first step to understanding is to quantify the Chinese and Japanese American IQ/achievement gaps and a prerequisite to that is deriving best estimates of the mean IQ of these two groups. The 16 IQ studies existent force us to focus on the post-war generation. Some studies are more reliable or more relevant to that generation than others and therefore, all studies must be ranked in those terms. Some of the best studies give IQ data only for "Orientals", do not distinguish between Chinese and Japanese, and therefore can only contribute toward global estimates for the two groups taken together. This poses the question of whether the same estimates can serve for Chinese and Japanese taken separately, or whether we must posit a certain mean IQ for Chinese Americans and another mean IQ for Japanese Americans.

RANKING IQ STUDIES

Most studies have been assigned a status of 1 to 4 going from most to least reliable. Status 1 was reserved for where a representative nationwide sample of Orientals or Chinese or Japanese was measured against a similar sample of American Whites. The Coleman Report of 1965 merits that status.

Status 2 was assigned where a good local sample of Chinese or Japanese was measured against a similar sample of Whites, or against nationwide White norms that inspire some confidence. Berkeley public schools (1968) had excellent local samples, Kauai Island (1965-1966) used the relatively reliable Stanford-Binet norms of 1932. Wyoming (1943-1945), where California Japanese were measured against Wyoming Whites, leaves open whether or not both groups were equally represented in their senior year but that probably made a difference of less than one point. The Chinatown (1972) sample was very small, but the subjects were resident in America prior to 1968 and were measured against WISC-R(W) norms. Project Talent (1960) also gets Status 2 although with some reservations: its initial sample was nationwide and excellent, but its respondent sample left a relatively small group of Orientals who were to some degree self-selected.

Status 3 was assigned to studies of a Chinese or Japanese sample in which that sample, or the White sample, or both suffered from a defect difficult to measure and correct. The best of these is Chinatown (1975) in which the uncertainty of the rate of obsolescence of Lorge-Thorndike norms is mitigated, at least somewhat, by a comparison with Bakersfield Whites. Hawaii (1960) and Los Angeles (1969-1970) both suffer from clearly substandard White samples: trying to distinguish Whites from Caucasians, or using Blacks rather than Whites to norm, are poor substitutes for sample quality. The best data from the Ethnic Minorities Research Project are the public school data from 1950 to 1969, but even those feature uncertainties about samples and tests that are collectively significant.

Status 4 designates studies in which the levelling effect of university attendance virtually guarantees samples unrepresentative of the general population. Western City (1977) is superior to the university students tested at Berkeley (1966), Southern California (1975-1976), and Hawaii (1978-1979) because its subjects met criteria set by a variety of universities rather than one only. Finally, a special bracketed status of (1) was given to the well-selected samples of Honolulu (1938), when Chinese and Japanese Americans were still unacculturated, and Westown (1985), by which time they had been overwhelmed by other Asian immigrants.

CHINESE AND JAPANESE IQ

Table 4.1 presents adjusted results for all studies from 1938 to 1985 with results for Chinese and Japanese merged rather than differentiated. It covers 16 studies with 11,373 subjects aged from 8 to 25 years and the studies are listed according to my estimates of their reliability. Others may prefer some

TABLE 4.1
Chinese and Japanese Americans: Mean IQs 1938 to 1985

Results of all studies

Study[a]	Year	N	Age (years)	Status[b]	IQ Nonverbal	IQ Verbal	IQ Overall
Coleman Report	1965	3995	8-17	1	99	95	97
Berkeley	1968	234	9–11	2	98	95	96
Kauai	1965-1966	253	9–10	2	99[c]	97[c]	98[c]
Wyoming	1943–1945	669	17	2	–	96	–
Chinatown	1972	53	9	2	101[c]	91[c]	96[c]
Project Talent	1960	150	17	2	97	96	96
Chinatown	1975	254	9–11	3	101[c]	89[c]	95[c]
Hawaii	1960–1963	554	15–17	3	–	96[c]	–
Los Angeles	1969–1970	390	16	3	99[c]	95[c]	97[c]
Ethnic Project	1950–1969	929	–	3	–	–	98
Western City	1977	98	25	4	99	92	96
Berkeley (U)	1966	309	18	4	–	94	–
S. California (U)	1975–1976	42	18–19	4	102	–	–
Hawaii (U)	1978–1979	118	20	4	101	98	99
Honolulu (E)	1938	3008	10–14	(1)	99	86	93
Westown (A)	1985	317	12–17	(1)	94	87	91

Estimates based on selected studies

Studies	Basis of estimate	N	IQ Nonverbal	IQ Verbal	IQ Overall
Status 2–3	Weighted average	3486	99.06	95.06	97.10
Status 2	Weighted average	1359	98.38	95.82	96.73
Coleman Report	Average grades 3-12	3995	98.63	95.01	96.82
Coleman Report	Grade 12 only	999	100.25	96.70	98.48

Note. Data from tables, Chapters 2–3; see text for full description of studies.

[a]Key to symbols: (U) = university students; (E) = subjects from an earlier period, that is, pre-war; (A) = Asian subjects from a later period with only a minority of Chinese and Japanese. [b]Key to status categories: 1–3 denote various degrees of reliability as described in text; 4 = samples selected by criteria that render them necessarily unrepresentative; (1) = well-selected samples of groups unrepresentative of Chinese and Japanese 1945–1975. [c]These values were substantially altered to adjust for either obsolete norms or sample bias.

other ranking but this really makes no difference because all studies, except the clearly unreliable or the least relevant, give similar results. It makes no difference whether or not you accept adjusted values. These have been identified with a raised letter "c" and those more skeptical than myself, say about adjustments for obsolescence, are invited to discard them and note the lack of effect.

Table 4.1 also presents summary estimates of the mean IQ of Chinese and Japanese Americans, two from the Coleman Report, two from all other studies assessed as having at least minimal reliability. The correspondence between all other studies taken collectively and grades 3 to 12 of the Coleman Report is remarkable, never differing by more than .81 points no matter whether one chooses only the more reliable studies (Status 2) or includes the less reliable as well (Status 2 plus Status 3). Therefore, these values might seem the obvious ones to accept and utilize. However, for reasons already stated, I use the slightly higher values from the Coleman Report 12th graders, primarily because they are the highest values and leave some margin for error. These give 100 for nonverbal IQ, 97 for verbal IQ, and 98.5 for overall IQ.

The summary estimates are based on mainstream IQ tests. There are a few studies in which Chinese outperform Whites, but all of these involve unusual tests. On a set of 25 map-reading tasks, Feldman (1971, p. 493) found that Chinese children aged 10 to 14 years outperformed Whites by .196 standard deviations, which would be equivalent to 2.94 IQ points. The test is difficult to classify as IQ or achievement because map skills were universally included in the school curricula (Feldman, 1971, p. 486). Tuddenham (1969) tested a small group of mainly Chinese children aged 6 to 10 years on 10 items based on Piaget's theory of cognitive development. The number of Oriental subjects who took each item varied from 17 to 29 and they scored .079 standard deviations above Whites, equivalent to 1.19 IQ points. Finally, as we saw under Berkeley (1968) and Chinatown (1975), Chinese children aged 5 to 10 years do unusually well on the Figure Copying Test. This consists of copying shapes such as diamonds, cylinders, and cubes, but it is not a mere drawing test. Rather it determines at what age children have conceptualized these figures (Jensen, 1980, pp. 663-664) and at least at grades 3 and 4, Chinese children are about one year ahead of White children.

I do not think these studies should affect our summary estimates. Chinese children may be able to perform certain cognitive tasks earlier than White children. However, there appear to be no sophisticated versions of these tasks that differentiate Chinese and White adolescents. And concerning mainstream IQ tests, at all ages, either such tasks are absent or a Chinese advantage on them is outweighed by worse performance on other cognitive tasks.

TABLE 4.2
Chinese and Japanese Americans: Mean IQs Compared

Study	Group	N	IQ Nonverbal	IQ Verbal	IQ Overall
Berkeley	Chinese[a]	234	98	95	96
Kauai	Japanese	253	99	97	98
Wyoming	Japanese	669	–	96	–
Chinatown (1972)	Chinese	53	101	91	96
Chinatown (1975)	Chinese	254	101	–	–
Hawaii	Chinese	64	–	96	–
	Japanese	490	–	96	–
Los Angeles	Japanese[b]	390	99	95	97
Ethnic Project	Chinese	806	–	–	98
	Japanese	123	–	–	99
Honolulu	Chinese	1352	98	–	–
	Japanese	1656	101	–	–
All studies[c]	Chinese	2763	99.30	94.70	97.47
	Japanese	3581	99.87	95.99	97.74

Note: Data from Tables 2.1, 2.2, 2.5, 3.1, 3.3, 3.5, 3.6, 3.7, and 3.8.

[a]Census data suggest ratio of 2.42 to 1 of Chinese over Japanese; [b]Census data suggest ratio of 2.60 to 1 of Japanese over Chinese; [c]IQ means for "All studies" calculated as follows: weighted means were calculated for California and Hawaii respectively; these were then combined using ratios, for Chinese 3.27 to 1 in favor of California, for Japanese 1.02 to 1 in favor of Hawaii.

CHINESE VERSUS JAPANESE IQ

Table 4.2 contains all studies that allow a comparison between Chinese and Japanese mean IQs. Since it is one of the few studies that gives separate results for both groups, I included the nonverbal scores from Honolulu (1938). I did not use the verbal scores because they were lowered by lack of acculturation. I included nonverbal scores from Chinatown (1975) but not verbal scores because they were lowered by recent immigrants. All unreliable or Status 4 studies were omitted. The studies listed contain no national samples but only local samples from Hawaii or California: the "Wyoming" Japanese are California Japanese in detention. Fortunately, even in 1970, 51% of Chinese Americans and 73% of Japanese Americans still lived in those two states. To get as good a regional profile as possible, I weighted the data as described at the bottom of the table.

Table 4.2 suggests that the mean IQs of Chinese and Japanese Americans are similar. The Japanese may have a one point advantage for verbal IQ but this does not translate into an advantage for overall IQ. The evidence on IQ variance is sparse (Flaughter, personal communication, August 13, 1987; Jensen, personal communication, August 27, 1987; Yee & La Forge, 1974). However, it suggests similar *SDs* and therefore, that our estimates for Chinese and Japanese taken together are roughly accurate for each group taken separately. The relevant values are nonverbal mean and *SD*, 100.25 and 18.07; verbal mean and *SD*, 96.70 and 15.41; overall mean and *SD*, 98.48 and 16.74. These values are not accurate to anything like two decimal places, but when estimates are rough, nothing is gained by rounding them off and making them rougher still.

IQ AND OCCUPATION

Having derived a best estimate of Chinese and Japanese mean IQ, we can address the problem of measuring the gap between their IQ and their achievements. I have chosen occupational status as the primary measure of group achievement because it is the closest thing to a universal criterion of achievement in our culture. According to Jensen (1980, p. 340), prestige rankings of occupations cut across men and women, old and young, upper and lower class, and have shown a remarkable persistence that spans at least three generations. Occupational status has other advantages: it ranks virtually the entire population and it provides a quantifiable link between group achievement and IQ. The link is forged by the fact that various occupations have IQ thresholds which correlate with their social status. For example, the threshold for the elite professions is so high that mainly the top 25% of Whites can qualify, the threshold for all managerial, professional, and technical occupations is such that only about the top 50% can qualify.

The ideal method would use the occupational achievements of Chinese (or Japanese) Americans to get an **estimated** IQ of this sort: a mean IQ which shows what IQ a subgroup of the White population would need to match their occupational achievements. We already have the **actual** IQ of Chinese Americans normed against White Americans. Therefore, the **difference** between their estimated and their actual IQ gives us exactly what we want: a measure of how much Chinese Americans overperform occupationally when compared to White Americans. For example, if Chinese Americans have an estimated IQ which is 20 points higher than their actual IQ, then that is the measure of their IQ/occupational achievement gap. This should make it clear that saying Chinese or Japanese "overperform" is not meant pejoratively. It merely means that they are more successful in terms of getting jobs most Whites value than Whites themselves are. Also note that our method confers a bonus. It makes use of a fiction, namely, it treats Chinese and Japanese Americans as if they could be identified with a subgroup of the White population. And if it shows that they actually perform very differently than Whites, then we will have to give up that fiction: in order to explain their overperformance, we will have to stop treating them like Whites and look to what makes them different.

Method

Gottfredson (1987) for occupations, Jensen (1973, pp. 231-234) for university admissions, use the same method: select an achievement with a known IQ threshold; use the mean IQ and *SD* of two groups to calculate what ratio should exist between them above that threshold; compare the estimated ratio to the actual ratio. For example, when Jensen applied this method to securing admission to America's better universities, he did the following: put the IQ threshold for admission at 117; used a mean IQ of 100 and *SD* of 15 to calculate that only the top 13% of Whites could qualify; used a mean IQ of 85 and *SD* of 13 to calculate that about 0.7% of Blacks could qualify. This gave an estimated per capita ratio of 18.6 to 1 in favor of Whites over Blacks. When adjusted to take account of the somewhat higher IQs of high school graduates, the estimated ratio was close to the actual ratio of White to Black for admission to these universities. Therefore, Jensen concluded that the match between IQ and achievement in this area was excellent.

My method is essentially the above method in reverse: take the actual per capita ratio of Chinese (or Japanese) to Whites who have secured entry to certain occupations; use the IQ threshold of those occupations, plus the *SDs* of Chinese and Whites, to estimate what mean IQ Chinese should have to attain that ratio; compare their estimated IQ to their actual IQ. This method is in accord with our overall method of measuring the Chinese IQ/achievement gap. It treats them as a subgroup of the White population known to have atypical IQ variance but whose mean IQ is unknown and must be estimated from their occupational achievements. As described, it requires IQ thresholds for various occupations, plus the per capita ratios of Chinese and Japanese to White in those occupations.

Thresholds

As we have seen, Weyl (1969) did a classic analysis of the 1960 census to establish the proportional contributions of American ethnic groups to high status occupations. Those he selected divide naturally into two groups, elite professions and a less exclusive group inclusive of all professions plus technicians. I wish to supplement Weyl's occupational categories with a larger one inclusive of all managerial, professional, and technical personnel. This category offers the most meaningful comparison of the occupational achievements of ethnic groups. First, it affords a comparison of substantial portions of the populations in question, for example, by 1980 about 43% of Chinese (with recent immigrants removed) and 27% of Whites pursued these occupations. Second, it is broad enough to include all occupations generally considered to have IQ thresholds at or above the White population mean. Third, it compensates for certain ethnic tendencies, such as the fact that Chinese tend to eschew managerial in favor of technical posts, whether by choice or because of discrimination (Hsia, 1988, p. 173).

Our task is to derive IQ thresholds for the preceding occupational categories. The most meaningful category, that inclusive of all managerial, professional, and technical personnel, includes a portion of the White population so large that we can use the method of correlational analysis. The correlation between IQ and occupational status is .50 to .60 for younger males, .70 for those over 40 years of age (Jensen, 1980, p. 341). This implies that all males 16 years and over should have a correlation of about .65 and that the same would be true of males aged 30 to 34. In 1980, 28% of employed White males 16 years and over had managerial, professional, or technical occupations (Bureau of the Census, 1980, PC80-1-D1-A, Table 280). The top 28% of the White IQ distribution has a mean of 118 and if there were a perfect correlation between occupation and IQ, the mean IQ of those who can qualify for these occupations would also be 118. But since the correlation is only .65, their mean IQ will be 111.7: the correlation is a measure of regression to the mean; and 18 x .65 = 11.7. The top 51% of the White IQ distribution has a mean of 111.7 and the top 51% fall above an IQ of 99.61. Therefore, 99.61 is our IQ threshold for these occupations.

Society keeps creating more and more managerial, professional, and technical posts and therefore, the proportion of the population holding such posts is rising. As the occupational category becomes less elite, its IQ threshold should tend to drop. The 1980 census shows that White males aged 30 to 34 years were more likely to hold such posts than older men, indeed, almost 35% of them did so (Bureau of the Census, 1980, PC80-1-

D1-A, Table 280). That percentage plus correlational analysis suggests an IQ threshold above which over 57% of them would fall, which gives an estimate of 97.25. I have used thresholds derived in this manner for all calculations relating to the managerial, professional, and technical category.

There is another more complex method of deriving IQ thresholds that requires actual IQ data for those who practice the relevant occupations. For example, the test scores of accountants, professors, scientists, and physicians allow an estimate of the threshold for the elite professions; that data plus scores for teachers and pharmacists allow an estimate for the less exclusive category of all professions plus technicians. The relevant data from Matarazzo (1972) suggest an IQ threshold of 110 for the elite professions, 100 for all professions plus technicans. Note how close the latter is to the value we derived from correlational analysis: the 99.61 for all ages 16 years and over who are managerial, professional, or technical personnel. It appears that managers also have an IQ threshold of about 100 and Matarazzo's data for them, while sparse, is consistent with that conclusion. The analysis of his data can be found in Appendix A.

Ratios and means

Weyl (1969, Table IV) gave occupational ratios of Chinese and Japanese to White based on the 1960 census. The 1980 census gives more detailed data and allows us to distinguish native born from foreign born, deduct immigrants in terms of year of arrival (post-1970 and post-1965), and focus on various age groups (Bureau of the Census, 1980, PC80-1-C1, Tables 125 &163; Bureau of the Census, 1980, PC80-1-D1-A, Table 280; East-West Center, 11 August 1988, Tables 13, 21, & 77; East-West Center, undated, Table 7, pp. 1361-1392 & 1473-1504).

The calculation of estimated mean IQs for Chinese and Japanese Americans from the relevant ratios and thresholds has been foreshadowed, but an example is given at the bottom of Table 4.3. The values used for the actual means and *SD*s of Chinese and Japanese are those from the 12th graders of the Coleman Report. The Coleman Report mean of 98.48 has been raised to 99 because the census gives occupational data for Whites as including 3% to 4% Hispanics: when Chinese and Japanese are normed on such a population, their mean IQ rises by half a point. The Coleman report *SD* of 16.74 has not been altered because so small an admixture of Hispanics would have virtually no effect.

Estimates

In Table 4.3, the actual IQs of Chinese and Japanese Americans have been subtracted from their estimated IQs based on occupational achievement. The difference is their IQ/achievement gap, for example, Chinese Americans circa 1980 overperformed vis-à-vis Whites by at least 15 IQ points. All those who arrived after 1970 have been eliminated from the occupational data because, it will be recalled, our IQ data are from Chinese and Japanese resident in America prior to 1970. Despite this, the match between those who earned the estimated IQs and those who earned the actual IQs is poor and in a moment, we will improve on this.

Table 4.3 may give only rough values but it allows for some interesting comparisons. The 1980 data are mainly for all employed persons aged 16 years and older so as to allow comparison to Weyl's 1960 data. Between 1960 and 1980, Chinese and Japanese IQ/occupational achievement gaps have been remarkably stable. Naturally, there have been trends affecting specific occupations. Since 1960, Chinese Americans have shown a strong tendency to abandon school-related occupations and where they remain in schools, they have left the classroom to become librarians and counsellors. Some will count this development as the most convincing piece of evidence ever adduced in favor of Chinese intelligence.

Chinese IQ/achievement gaps are much larger than the Japanese gaps. The most meaningful comparison is for the category embracing all professions, technical posts, and managerial posts, which covers substantial percentages of both populations. In 1980, Chinese overperformed by 15 IQ points, Japanese by only 5 IQ points. However, Japanese who were aged 25 to 44 years in 1980 show a sizable gap of 9 IQ points; it is those aged 45 to 70 years who pull the estimates down. The latter group was aged 7 to 32 years in 1942 when fully 45% of Japanese Americans suffered the trauma of evacuation from their homes into relocation centers. Perhaps school age children suffered from interrupted education and young adults from interrupted careers. At any rate, those aged 25 to 44 years in 1980 are far more representative of our target group, the generation born or reared since World War II.

Table 4.3 also gives estimates for Chinese and Japanese Americans who are native born, that is, born in America. This is in response to Hsia (1988, pp. 160-161) who shows that overrepresentation of Asian Americans in certain occupations, such as science and engineering, has always been due primarily to the foreign born. Her data suggested the hypothesis that the high occupational profile of Chinese and Japanese Americans was dependent on a continual influx of immigrants, born and educated overseas, and did not persist in the American environment, among those born and educated in the United States. In fact native-born Chinese outperform foreign-born Chinese

TABLE 4.3
Chinese and Japanese Americans 1960 and 1980
Difference Between Actual IQ and IQ Estimated on the Basis of Occupation

Occupations	Threshold[a]	Ratio[b]	IQ Estimated[c]	Actual[d]	Difference
		Chinese 1960			
Elite professions	110	2.264	113	99	14
Professions & technical	100	1.766	120	99	21
		Chinese 1980 (resident pre-1970)			
Elite professions	110	2.433	114	99	15
Professions & technical	100	1.793	121	99	22
Professions, technical and managerial	100	1.584	114	99	15
		Chinese 1980 (native born)			
Professions, technical and managerial	100	1.526	113	99	14
		Japanese 1960			
Elite professions	110	1.228	102	99	3
Professions & technical	100	1.299	106	99	7
		Japanese 1980 (resident pre-1970)			
Elite professions	110	1.367	103	99	4
Professions & technical	100	1.236	105	99	6
Professions, technical and managerial	100	1.161	104	99	5
		Japanese 1980 (ages 25 to 44 and resident pre-1970)			
Professions, technical and managerial	98	1.305	108	99	9
		Japanese 1980 (ages 25 to 44 and native born)			
Professions, technical and managerial	98	1.361	109	99	10

[a]The threshold gives an IQ above which about 90% of those in each occupational category would score. [b]The ratio is the per capita ratio of Chinese or Japanese to White in each occupational category. [c]Estimated IQ refers to means for Chinese or Japanese Americans in general calculated from the thresholds and ratios (see below). [d]Actual IQ is the mean for the 12th graders of the Coleman Report.

Chinese 1980, Professions, technical, and managerial, Estimated IQ: (1) White mean and SD = 100 and 15; (2) 99.61 (IQ threshold) is .026 SDs (.39 ÷ 15 = .026) below White mean; (3) Percentage of Whites above 99.61 = 51.035%; (4) 51.035% x 1.584 = 80.84 as percentage of Chinese above 99.61; (5) Chinese mean is .872 SDs above 99.61; (6) .872 x 16.74 (Chinese SD) = 14.60 as IQ points to be added to 99.61; (7) 99.61 + 14.60 = 114.21 or **114** as estimated IQ.

in terms of occupational achievement. It should be said that post-1970 Chinese immigrants have a lower occupational profile and when they are removed, the foreign born gain a one-point advantage. Native-born Japanese outperform foreign-born Japanese and here, there is no ambiguity. Japanese immigrants since 1970 have been an elite and therefore, when they are removed, the native born retain their higher occupational profile. Native-born Japanese aged 25 to 44 years in 1980 opened up an IQ/achievement gap of fully 10 points.

Best Estimates

Thus far, we have analyzed mainly those who were aged 16 years and over at the time of the 1960 census, or at the time of the 1980 census. If we take those who had achieved the occupation of their maturity, those aged 30 years and over, the 1960 data give the occupational achievements of people who had left school before 1948. Most of those from the 1980 census, those aged 38 years and over, had left school before 1960. Yet, our estimates for the actual IQs of Chinese and Japanese come from those who were school children during the 1960s. The match between IQ and achievement is clearly poor. Perhaps the actual IQs of Chinese and Japanese drop as we go back into the past; perhaps their occupational achievements are moving upward, so that young Chinese and Japanese had a better profile in 1980 than older age groups. If so, the values for the IQ/achievement gaps in Table 4.3 would tend to be low. In order to get a good data match between school-tested IQ and eventual adult occupations, we will follow the Coleman Report 12th graders through to their 1980 occupations, and compare **their** estimated IQs with **their** actual IQs.

Table 4.4 achieves all of this. The Coleman Report 12th graders were aged 17-18 years in 1965 and by 1980, they were aged 32-33: therefore, Table 4.4 takes the occupational profile of ages 30-34 from the 1980 census and removes all those who arrived in America after 1965. Therefore, it at least simulates following the Coleman Report cohorts from IQ testing as high school seniors to their occupational achievements as adults. It also uses IQ thresholds appropriate to these cohorts, thresholds which take into account the increased number of young adults in high status occupations by 1980. The Chinese total cohort has an IQ/achievement gap of 21 points, one point lower for the native born, and the Japanese total cohort a gap of 10 points, one point higher for the native born. These constitute our best estimates of the Chinese and Japanese IQ/occupational achievement gaps, estimates that I usually round off to 20 and 10 points respectively.

TABLE 4.4

Coleman Report Cohorts: Difference Between Actual IQ As 12th Graders (1965) and
IQ Estimated on the Basis of Occupation 15 Years Later (1980)

Group	Threshold[a]	Ratio[b]	IQ Estimated[c]	Actual	Difference
Chinese total cohort[d]	97	1.588	120	99	21
Chinese native born[e]	97	1.572	119	99	20
Japanese total cohort[d]	97	1.323	109	99	10
Japanese native born[e]	97	1.345	110	99	11

[a]The threshold applies to Americans, aged 30 to 34 years in 1980, who were in managerial, professional, and technical occupations; it gives an IQ above which about 90% of them would score. [b]The ratio applies to those members of the groups listed who, in 1980, were aged 30 to 34 years and in the occupational categories named; it gives the per capita ratio of Chinese or Japanese to White. [c]Estimated IQ refers to mean IQs for the groups listed calculated from the thresholds and ratios (see below). [d]Total cohort refers to all Chinese and Japanese Americans who were 12th graders in American high schools in 1965. [e]Native born refers to the American born members of the total cohorts.

Example of calculations, estimated IQ of Chinese total cohort:

(1) White mean and SD = 100 and 15; (2) 97.25 (IQ threshold) is .183 SDs (2.75 + 15 = .183) below White mean; (3) Percentage of Whites above 97.25 = 57.26%; (4) 57.26% x 1.5876 (Chinese to White ratio) gives 90.91 as percentage of Chinese above 97.25; (5) Chinese mean is 1.335 SDs above 97.25; (6) 1.335 x 16.74 (Chinese SD) = 22.35 as IQ points to be added to 97.25; (7) 97.25 + 22.35 = 119.60 or **120** as estimated IQ.

IQ AND INCOME

There is a positive correlation between IQ and income, albeit much lower than that between IQ and occupation. The purpose of the next section is to compare the actual IQs of Chinese and Japanese Americans with the estimated IQs we would posit based on their incomes.

Method

As usual, Chinese and Japanese are treated as if they were a subgroup of the White population. First, as if they had been raised in typical White homes, typical that is for parental factors that influence what income children will earn as adults. Second, as if despite this equality of family background, they grew up to attain higher than average adult incomes. And as usual, their mean IQ as schoolchildren is treated as an unknown which must be estimated from the effect of IQ on income within White America, that is, its effect when family background is held constant. The assumption that the postwar generation of Chinese and Japanese Americans were raised in homes roughly equal to Whites is based on fact. Between 1945 and 1965, their formative years, their parents gradually went from below Whites to above Whites on an index including occupation, education, and income (Petersen, 1971, p. 121).

Income data

The 1980 census gives the median income of full-time workers in 1979 (Bureau of the Census, 1980, PC80-1-C1, Tables 164 & 170; Bureau of the Census, 1980, PC80-1-D1-A, Table 295). Since ethnic groups differ in terms of holding part-time jobs, full-time workers provide the best comparative index. Once again, all Chinese and Japanese who had arrived after 1970 were removed (East-West Center, undated, Table 11, pp. 261-262, 264-265, 282-283, 285-286; East-West Center, 11 August 1988, Tables 21 & 65). About 83% of recent Chinese immigrants were born in mainland China, Hong Kong, or Taiwan and those born elsewhere were assumed to be similar, on the basis of the occupational data cited in the section on occupation.

Because Chinese and Japanese have more female full-time workers than Whites, median incomes for the sexes were calculated separately and then combined in terms of the White sex ratio. Unfortunately, there is no age-related data available for recent immigrants. However, using full-time workers does much to equate these groups for age: Chinese median age was virtually identical to White; Japanese males were virtually identical but Japanese females about four years older than White females. Since Japanese income was not much affected by recent immigrants, who were fewer than 10% of full-time workers, a rough calculation could be done equating their age distribution with White. This resulted in an adjustment of less than $150, so the medians presented for all groups can be taken as approximating age-adjusted values.

Chinese and Japanese Americans are more likely to live in areas in which Whites have above average incomes. Despite this, I have not adjusted White income upward because actually, this would undermine the match between income and IQ. With one or two exceptions, our best IQ data norm Chinese and Japanese on Whites nationwide; therefore, we must "norm" their income on Whites nationwide. To reinforce the point, the areas that show Whites with higher than average incomes also show Whites with higher than average IQs. So if the former were to be adjusted upward, the latter would have to be adjusted upward as well, so as to restore the match. I suspect the two adjustments would cancel out, but until someone provides an IQ map that fits the American income map, we cannot really know. Finally, in accord with my overall method, no adjustments have been made for ethnic factors, such as lower income for Chinese due to discrimination overt or covert (Hsia, 1988, pp. 183-202).

Examples of Calculations

Jencks (1972, p. 346) used path analysis to estimate the effect of IQ on income for Whites with family background held constant. Taking IQ measured at 11 years of age, he derived path coefficients with income ranging from .194 to .232, giving .213 as the mid-point. If we wish to use the IQ difference between two White groups from equivalent backgrounds to estimate incomes, the coefficient must be used as a multiplier. The IQ difference (in standard deviation units) times .213 will give the estimated income difference in standard deviation units; and when that is taken times $9,497, the *SD* for the incomes of White full-time workers in 1979, it gives the estimated income difference in dollars. If we wish to use the income difference between two such groups to estimate their IQ difference, the coefficient must be used as a divisor. First use the *SD* of $9,497 to reduce the dollar difference to an *SD* difference and take that times 15 (the White *SD* for IQ); when that is divided by .213, it gives the estimated IQ difference in IQ points.

Examples of the calculations are given at the bottom of Table 4.5. The value for the *SD* of White full-time workers was calculated from those whose incomes fell between $10,000 and $25,000. Below this range, the minimum wage reduces variance and above it, those few with huge incomes enormously expand variance.

TABLE 4.5
Chinese, Japanese, and White Americans 1979: IQ and Income

Difference between actual income and income estimated by IQ

		Income		
Group	IQ	Estimated	Actual[a]	Difference
White	100.0	15 704	15 704	–
Chinese	98.5	15 502	17 668	2 166
Japanese	98.5	15 502	17 364	1 862

Difference between actual IQ and IQ estimated by income

		IQ		
Group	Income[b]	Estimated	Actual	Difference
Chinese	103.1	114.6	98.5	16.1
Japanese	102.6	112.3	98.5	13.8
White	100.0	100.0	100.0	–

[a]Median income of full-time workers, Chinese and Japanese resident pre-1970; adjusted in terms of White sex ratio and age distribution—see text. [b]The actual incomes have been translated into values analogous to IQ scores, that is, the mean for White income was set at 100, the *SD* at 15.

Examples of calculations:

Chinese estimated income: (1) 100.0 (White mean) – 98.5 (Chinese mean) = 1.5; (2) 1.5 ÷ 15 (White *SD*) = .10 *SDU;* (3) .10 x .213 (path coefficient between IQ and income) = .0213 *SDU;* (4) .0213 x $9497 (White *SD*) = $202; (5) $15 704 (White median) – 202 = **$15 502**.

Chinese estimated IQ: (1) $17 668 (Chinese median) – 15 704 (White median) = $1964; (2) $1964 ÷ 9497 (White *SD*) = .207 *SDU* ; (3) .207 x 15 (White *SD*) = 3.10; (4) 3.10 ÷ .213 (path coefficient between IQ and income) = 14.6; (5) 14.6 + 100 (White mean) = **114.6**.

Estimates

Table 4.5 shows that the mean IQ of Chinese and Japanese Americans badly underestimates their incomes: Chinese earn almost $2,200 more than predicted and Japanese almost $1,900. Both groups have had their median incomes boosted by adjustments. The Chinese went from parity with American Whites to $2,000 above, primarily after removal of post-1970 immigrants, but with a small gain from being equated with the White sex ratio. The Japanese went from $1,100 above Whites to $1,700 above, primarily because of the sex ratio factor, with some of that gain lost by adjustment for age. The removal of those who arrived between 1970 and 1980 was dictated by the IQ data available but most recent immigrants are at a great disadvantage in terms of income, so their removal has the added benefit of a fairer comparison between Chinese and Whites. The Japanese were not much affected by this because their recent immigrants have been few and elite.

Table 4.5 puts the Chinese IQ/achievement gap based on income at 16 points. This is one point higher than the estimate based on their representation in professional, technical, and managerial occupations in Table 4.3. These two estimates are the appropriate ones to compare because they cover essentially the same age groups: all those 15 years and over as compared to all those 16 and over. The Japanese estimate based on income is 13.8 IQ points. This is greater than all the occupational estimates, even the 10-point estimate from the Coleman Report cohort (Table 4.4). Japanese occupational estimates approach their income estimate only when those most affected by relocation centers are removed from the former but not the latter. Perhaps the World War II evacuation did more to restrict entry into high status occupations than it did to reduce the capacity to make money.

THE IQ/ACHIEVEMENT GAP

It may be unfair to Japanese Americans but I will not revise our occupational estimates upward, despite the higher values based on income. Income really provides only a rough check on occupational achievement: the path coefficient between income and IQ is very low and the path analysis rests on a number of problematic assumptions (Jencks, 1972, pp. 345-346). Therefore, our best estimates of the size of the IQ/achievement gaps remain unchanged: 20 points for Chinese, 10 points for Japanese. Whatever the exact size of these gaps, their very existence shows that ignoring ethnic differences between Chinese, Japanese, and White Americans does not work. A group of Whites with the same mean IQ as Chinese Americans would fall far below their achievements; a group of Whites with the same achievements as Chinese Americans would have a much higher mean IQ. We must analyze the developmental process that culminates in the achievements of Chinese and Japanese Americans and that analysis will have to focus on the cultural distance that separates these two groups from the White majority.

5

The Two Factors
of Overachievement

The path by which Chinese and Japanese overachieve compared to White Americans begins with achievement tests at school, passes through the Scholastic Aptitude Test (SAT) and university entrance, passes through the Graduate Record Exam (GRE) and entry into graduate or professional schools, and culminates in their high occupational profile. However, to follow that path we need a guide in the form of working hypotheses. These can be derived by making explicit the assumptions that generate the Chinese and Japanese IQ/occupational achievement gaps; and stating hypotheses that challenge those assumptions.

First, the assumptions: Chinese, Japanese, and White Americans have the same IQ thresholds for various occupational categories; all three groups capitalize on those who meet the thresholds to the same degree. Second, two hypotheses that challenge those assumptions: Chinese and Japanese have lower IQ thresholds than Whites, for example, Chinese might qualify for a high status occupation with an IQ of 90 although Whites needed an IQ of 97; Chinese and Japanese have higher capitalization rates than Whites. By the latter, I mean that something like 78% of those who fall above the Chinese threshold for managerial, professional, and technical posts might in fact enter those occupations, although the figure for Whites was only 60%. In other words, thanks to a lower threshold, the Chinese may have a larger pool of those with the requisite IQ than we would expect; and as a group, the Chinese may capitalize on that pool of talent more effectively than Whites capitalize on their own pool.

OCCUPATION REVISITED

For these two hypotheses to be viable, they must explain the extraordinary ratios of Chinese or Japanese to Whites in high status occupations. These ratios are based on the fact that those who follow those occupations are a much higher percentage of the Chinese population than the White population. For example, in Table 4.4, the ratio of 1.588 Chinese for each White is based on the fact that 54.68% of the Chinese cohort had a managerial, professional, or technical post, whereas only 34.44% of Whites did (54.68 ÷ 34.44 = 1.588). When we account for those 54.68% by positing a special Chinese capitalization rate and a special IQ threshold, the two interact: the higher the capitalization rate, the closer the Chinese threshold can be to the White threshold.

Assume that the Chinese capitalized on literally everyone above their IQ threshold. This would generate a threshold that cut off 54.68% of their Coleman Report cohort. And that would put the threshold only marginally below the Chinese mean IQ which, when the fact Whites include 4% Hispanics is taken into account, stands at 99. In fact, the threshold would be 97.07, or virtually identical to the White threshold of 97.25. That assumption is of course absurd, that is, no group could hope that everyone above their IQ threshold for high status occupations would actually enter those occupations. On the other hand, assume that the Chinese capitalization rate was no higher than the White rate which stands at just over 60%. Then their IQ threshold would have to bear the entire burden of explaining their IQ/achievement gap, and we would have to posit a threshold that cut off 90.91% of their Coleman Report cohort (54.68 ÷ 60.15 = 90.91%). And that would put the Chinese threshold more than 20 points below the White threshold of 97.25. Which means that our second assumption, of no difference between Chinese and White capitalization rates, is equally absurd. It would have Chinese qualifying for high status occupations with IQs as low as 77.

It should now be evident that by manipulating the capitalization rate, we can generate IQ thresholds for Chinese and Japanese within a wide range. There is no data on what percentage of these groups above a certain IQ actually go into high status occupations and, indeed, such data would be very difficult to come by. However, there is data relevant to their IQ thresholds and therefore, I have simply put the capitalization rate at whatever

TABLE 5.1

Chinese, Japanese, and White Americans 1980

Hypothesized Capitalization Rates and IQ Thresholds for Various Occupational Categories

Group	Capitalization rate[a]	Threshold[b]	Distance below White threshold[c]
Coleman Report cohorts: Managerial, professional, and technical			
White	60	97.25	–
Chinese	78	90.25	7.00
Japanese	74	94.25	3.00
Ages 16 and over (resident pre-1970): Elite professions			
White	25	110.00	–
Chinese	37	103.00	7.00
Japanese	26	107.00	3.00

[a]A group's membership in an occupational category expressed as a percentage of those above that group's IQ threshold for that occupational category. [b]The threshold gives an IQ above which about 90% in each occupational category would score. [c]How far the Chinese (or Japanese) threshold is below the White threshold expressed in IQ points.

Example of calculations, Coleman Report cohorts, Chinese:

(1) 54.68% of Chinese cohort were in managerial, professional, or technical occupations; (2) Assume that they represented 78% of those above Chinese IQ threshold; (3) Then 70.02% were above that threshold (54.68 ÷ 70.02 = 78.09%); (4) That threshold is .525 SDs below Chinese mean IQ; (5) .525 x 16.74 (Chinese SD) = 8.79 IQ points to be subtracted from Chinese mean; (6) Chinese mean (normed against Whites with 4% Hispanics) = 99.04; and (7) 99.04 − 8.79 = **90.25** as Chinese threshold.

value generates the appropriate threshold. So the viability of my hypotheses concerning the Chinese and Japanese IQ/occupational achievement gaps depends upon two things: whether the evidence suggests the thresholds I posit; and, as a sort of check, whether the capitalization rates that generate those thresholds are plausible.

Table 5.1 gives a preview of what IQ thresholds can be evidenced, that is, Chinese thresholds 7 points below White and Japanese thresholds 3 points below White. For the managerial, professional, and technical category, it uses 1980 data for the Coleman Report cohorts. As Table 5.1 shows, plausible capitalization rates generate the appropriate thresholds: Chinese,

Japanese, and Whites get rates of 78%, 74%, and 60% respectively. An example of the calculations appears at the bottom of the table. There is no Coleman Report data for the elite professions, so I used census data for employed persons aged 16 years and over, Chinese and Japanese resident in America prior to 1970. Here again, Table 5.1 shows that plausible capitalization rates generate the appropriate thresholds: Chinese, Japanese, and Whites get 37%, 26%, and 25% respectively.

It remains to determine whether Chinese IQ thresholds 7 points below White, and Japanese thresholds 3 points below White, tally with the evidence. Academic achievement plays a major role in securing entry into high status occupations. If Chinese and Japanese have lower IQ thresholds for those occupations, we would expect that they can match the academic achievements of Whites despite lower IQs. Achievement tests taken at school should give us our first glimpse of the evolution of lower thresholds.

ACHIEVEMENT TESTS

When analyzing comparative studies of Asian and White American IQ, several with achievement test data were singled out. These include every study which meets the following criteria: Chinese subjects or Japanese subjects or both and White subjects took IQ tests as well as achievement tests; the subjects were primarily from grades 3 to 12; the subjects were tested during the 1960s, that is, recently but prior to 1970. Table 5.2 contains these studies and since there is little differential data, treats Chinese and Japanese Americans collectively. In each case, their IQ score was subtracted from their achievement test score and the result labelled "Difference." Since both scores were normed on the same group of Whites, "Difference" shows: how much Chinese/Japanese outperform Whites on achievement tests when matched with Whites for IQ; or conversely, the extent to which Chinese/Japanese can match Whites on achievement tests despite lower IQs.

Table 5.2 shows several trends. First, Chinese and Japanese students open up an IQ/achievement test gap as they go from grade school to high school. Second, at high school, their nonverbal IQ/mathematics gap is greater than their verbal IQ/English gap. Finally, the more achievement tests deviate from IQ tests and move toward testing for school-taught subjects, particularly grammar and advanced mathematics, the larger the gaps become.

In Table 5.2, the IQ/achievement differences for high school students have been averaged to get overall estimates. All studies give 5.95 points for nonverbal IQ/mathematics and 3.40 points for verbal IQ/English, or about 4.7 points altogether. Omitting the Coleman Report gives 8.31 and 5.05 points respectively, or about 6.7 points altogether. The case for omitting the Coleman Report depends on whether what they called achievement tests, tests from the STEP series, were really little more than IQ tests and I believe that proposition can be defended (Anastasi, 1968, pp. 397 & 400; Mittman, 1965, pp. 880-881).

However, whether the Coleman Report results are omitted or included is not very important. They affect the exact size of the Table 5.2 IQ/achievement gap which is something less significant than its very existence. The size of the gap lacks social significance because the tests involved are not the ones actually used to screen for higher education or high status occupations. The Scholastic Aptitude Test and the Graduate Record Exam are used for that purpose and it would be fortuitous if the tests in Table 5.2, taken together, duplicated the mix of measuring IQ and measuring school learning found on the SAT and GRE. On the other hand, the existence of the Table 5.2 IQ/achievement gap helps prove a point. Much of our evidence for a Chinese or Japanese performance gap between IQ tests and achievement tests rests on assumptions about the mean IQ of Chinese and Japanese Americans in general. The Table 5.2 gap is based on the differential performance of subjects who took both kinds of tests at the same time, and therefore has nothing to do with assumptions about the population in general. Since estimates of the population mean IQ are rough, evidence not dependent on those estimates is highly desirable.

Concerning our primary interest, the evolution of lower IQ thresholds for Chinese and Japanese, Table 5.2 suggests a distance below Whites of at least 5 points, which could of course break down into 7 points for Chinese and 3 points for Japanese. Moreover, the IQ/achievement test gap does not in itself suffice to determine IQ thresholds. The trend toward higher values as school-taught subjects are approached suggests the existence of another gap, an IQ/school grades gap, which may be considerably higher than 5 points. Both are relevant because, after all, universities do not admit students on test scores alone but on a combination of test scores, school grades, and other factors.

TABLE 5.2
Chinese and Japanese Americans 1960–1970
Difference Between IQ and Achievement Test Scores

Level and Tests	Study	Difference[a]	Achievement Test[b]
Grade school Nonverbal IQ & math	Coleman Report	−1.53	STEP: Grasp concepts independent of school curriculum
	Berkeley	+0.58	SAT: School-taught arithmetical computation & applications
Grade school Verbal IQ & English	Coleman Report	+1.57	STEP: Drawing inferences from passages of prose & poetry
	Berkeley	+3.89	SAT: Spelling, punctuation, grammar, word & paragraph meaning
High school Nonverbal IQ & math	Coleman Report	−1.13	STEP: Grasp concepts independent of school curriculum
	Los Angeles	+3.58	QC: Comparing pairs of quantities for equality & inequality
	Hawaii (L)	+2.72/4.00[c]	SCAT & CAT: School-taught arithmetical computations & problems
	Hawaii (N)	+9.14[c]	SCAT: School-taught arithmetical computations & problems
	Project Talent	+15.11	MAT: Fractions, decimals, algebra, analytic geometry, & calculus
High school Verbal IQ & English	Coleman Report	+0.11	STEP: Drawing inferences from passages of prose & poetry
	Los Angeles	+3.18	SENT: Detect errors of language, punctuation, & capitalization
	Project Talent	+6.91	ENG: Language, punctuation, spelling, & capitalization

		Average differences	
Level	Tests	All studies	Coleman Report omitted
High School	Nonverbal IQ & math	+5.95	+8.31
	Verbal IQ & English	+3.40	+5.05

[a]Difference = achievement test score minus IQ – data from Tables 2.3, 2.4, 3.3, 3.5, and 3.6. [b]Tests: STEP = Sequential Tests of Educational Progress, 1955–1957; SAT = Stanford Achievement Tests, 1964, Intermediate I and II; QC = Quantitative Comparison test, Project Access; SCAT = Cooperative School and College Ability Test, 1955, Form 2A; CAT = California Ability Test, 1957, advanced Mathematics Test Form X; MAT = Mathematical factor, Project Talent, based on tests R-312 and R-333; SENT = Sentences test, Project Access; ENG = English language factor, Project Talent, based on tests R-231 to R-235. [c]The paired values are for SCAT and CAT, local norms, and were averaged to get a local estimate; the third value is for SCAT, national norms, and was averaged with the local estimate to get an overall Hawaii estimate.

THE SCHOLASTIC APTITUDE TEST

A university education is not absolutely essential for those who aspire to managerial, professional, or technical occupations. However, it is certainly a semi-prerequisite and, for many Americans, a serious intention to attend university means taking the Scholastic Aptitude Test-Verbal (SAT-V) and the Scholastic Aptitude Test-Mathematical (SAT-M). Hsia (1983, p. 131; 1988; pp. 25-26) gave results from 1971-1972 for both Asians and Whites and noted that 90% of the Asians were U.S. citizens. Since few become naturalized within five years of arrival, the preponderance of U.S. citizens plus university attendance rates for various Asian groups reveal much about the Asians in question: 99% of them had arrived in America by 1970; and about 80% of them were Chinese or Japanese. This makes them the best match for our target population of any SAT candidate group for whom differential data exist. Beginning in 1975-1976, separate results for Asians and Whites were published on a regular basis but by then, fewer candidates were Chinese or Japanese and fewer still were resident pre-1970 (Bureau of the Census, 1970, PC(2)-IG, Tables 2, 3, 17, 18, 32, & 33; East-West Center, 11 August 1988, Tables 77 & 79; East-West Center, undated, Table 11, pp. 261, 264, 282, 285, & 330; Gardner, Robey, & Smith, 1985, pp. 14-15).

The main drift of the 1971-1972 SAT results is quite unambiguous. Asian candidates who were mainly Chinese and Japanese Americans almost matched the performance of White Americans on the SAT. Asian candidates represented about 50% of the relevant cohort and White candidates represented under 30% of the relevant cohort. This means that the Asians were a much less elite group with a lower mean IQ and therefore, we know that Chinese and Japanese can match Whites on the SAT despite lower IQ. But what is the magnitude of the Asian overperformance? It is easy to formulate a method which will quantify their superiority but unfortunately, that method uses certain key values that can only be estimated. However, the estimates are plausible and even a rough measure may be preferable to simply describing Asian overperformance as "sizable" or "significant".

Method

 Our overall plan is to compare Asian and White performances on the SAT, get estimates of the mean IQs of the Asian and White candidates, and then calculate how many IQ points Asians can spot Whites and yet match them on the SAT.
 Comparing the SAT performance of Asians and Whites is easy. We need only convert SAT scores onto a scale analogous to IQ scores and that requires only one key value, a White population *SD* expressed in SAT points. Give that *SD* a value of 15 and you have commensurate SAT and IQ scores. Estimating the mean IQs of the Asian and White candidates, namely, those who sat the SAT in 1971-1972, is complex and it requires a number of key values.   Most of these would not be of general interest and their derivation can be found in Appendix B. There is one exception: Appendix B yields a correlation between actually taking the SAT and performance on the SAT; for the curious, the values are .65 for the SAT-V and .72 for the SAT-M.
 Once we have what we need, both the mean IQs and analogous SAT scores of Asian and White candidates, calculating Asian overperformance on the SAT is a matter of simple arithmetic. For example, assume the Asian candidates were 1 point above Whites on the SAT-M, but 4 points below them for nonverbal IQ. Clearly the performance difference is 5 points, that is, clearly these Asians could match Whites on the SAT-M despite an IQ deficit of 5 points.

Results

Table 5.3 compares Asians who were mainly pre-1970 Japanese and Chinese with Whites for performance on the SAT. The results are labelled "Difference" and show that: when Asians are equated with Whites for SAT-M scores, their nonverbal IQ is 5 points below Whites; when equated for SAT-V scores, their verbal IQ is about 4 points below; the average for overall IQ is 4.45 points. These results are a good match for those derived from achievement test data - see the estimates under "All studies" in Table 5.2.

TABLE 5.3
Asian and White Americans 1971–1972
Difference Between IQ and Scholastic Aptitude Test (SAT) Scores

	Nonverbal IQ		SAT-Math	IQ/SAT
White	Asian[a]	Deficit	Credit[b]	Difference[c]
110.94	107.25	3.69	(+)1.38	5.07 = 44 SAT points

	Verbal IQ		SAT-Verbal	IQ/SAT
White	Asian	Deficit	Deficit	Difference
109.11	101.29	7.82	(-)4.00	3.82 = 31 SAT points

	Overall IQ		SAT Average	IQ/SAT
White	Asian	Deficit	Deficit	Difference
110.03	104.27	5.76	(-)1.31	4.45

[a]Asians were approximately 41% Japanese, 39% Chinese, 10% Filipino, and 10% other, mainly Korean and Asian Indian. [b]Values for Asian credit (mean above White) or deficit (mean below White) on the SAT are analogous to IQ scores, that is, the White SD has been put at 15; a SAT credit must be added to an IQ deficit because it shows that Asians were above Whites on the SAT despite lower IQ; a SAT deficit must be subtracted from an IQ deficit because it shows Asians were below Whites on the SAT as well as for IQ (though not as far below). [c]Difference shows first, how many IQ points Asians fall below Whites when the two groups are matched for SAT scores; and second, how many SAT points Asians rise above Whites when matched for IQ.

Example of calculations, nonverbal IQ/SAT-M difference:

I.   White nonverbal IQ: (1) 27.5% sat SAT = 1.215 SDs above population mean; (2) Correlation between sitting SAT-M and nonverbal IQ = .60; (3) 1.215 x .60 = .729 $SDs;$ (4) .729 x 15 = 10.94 IQ points to be added to White mean; (5) 100 + **110.94** as nonverbal IQ of White SAT takers.

II.   Asian nonverbal IQ: (1) 52% sat SAT = .7671 $SDs;$ (2) Correlation as above = .60; (3) .7671 x .60 = .4603 $SDs;$ (4) .4603 x 18.07 (Asian SD for non-verbal IQ) = 8.32 points; (5) 98.93 (Asian nonverbal mean IQ with this mix of Asian groups) + 8.32 = **107.25** as nonverbal IQ of Asian SAT takers.

III.   Asian nonverbal IQ deficit: 110.94 – 107.25 = **3.69.**

IV.   Asian SAT-M credit: (1) 517 (Asian mean SAT-M) – 505 (White mean) = 12; (2) White SD for SAT-M = 130; (3) 12 + 130 = .0923 $SDs;$ (4) .0923 x 15 = **1.38.**

V.   Difference in IQ points: 3.69 + 1.38 = **5.07.**

VI.   Differences in SAT points: (1) 5.07 + 15 = .3380 $SDs;$ (2) .3380 x 130 = **44.**

Key values, verbal IQ/SAT-V difference:

(1) Correlation between sitting SAT-V and verbal IQ = .50; (2) Asian SD for verbal IQ = 15.41; (3) Asian verbal mean IQ with this mix of Asian groups = 95.38; (4) White SAT-V mean = 474; (5) Asian SAT-V mean = 442; (6) White SD for SAT-V = 120.

As emphasized, the SAT data have only speculative status and the results should be regarded as no more than reasonable hypotheses. So as to make these precise enough to be tested, the IQ "Difference" in Table 5.3 has been translated into a SAT "Difference." I predict: when Chinese plus Japanese are equated with White Americans for nonverbal IQ, they will outscore Whites by 44 SAT-M points; when equated for verbal IQ, the margin will be 31 SAT-V points. Strictly speaking, these hypotheses lapsed when the flood of post-1968 immigrants began to dominate but I suspect the situation is much the same today.

THE NATIONAL LONGITUDINAL STUDY

This study provides a valuable check on our SAT estimates. In the spring of 1972, the Educational Testing Service administered a battery of tests to a nationwide sample of high school seniors. They chose 18 randomly selected subjects from 1,200 randomly selected schools for a total of 21,600 students. The number actually tested was 16,683 and 94% of these designated their ethnicity, including 12,180 Whites and 182 Asian Americans. Hsia (1988, p. 27) supplied means and *SDs* for Whites and Asians on the NLS mathematics, vocabulary, and reading tests, and I used these to convert Asian/White performance gaps into scores analogous to IQ scores; that is, the White *SD* was set at 15. The converted mathematics score gives a NLS-Mathematics result, the vocabulary and reading scores were averaged to get a NLS-Verbal result.

The NLS results have one great advantage over our SAT results. With an excellent sample of high school seniors, and with estimates of Chinese and Japanese IQ normed on White high school seniors from the Coleman Report, Asian/White IQ comparisons are more straightforward. On the other hand, the NLS sample takes us farther away from our target group. The self-selection of SAT candidates favored Chinese and Japanese and pre-1970 residents, but the NLS sample was representative rather than self-selected. A representative sample of Asian high school seniors in 1972 would have only 65% Chinese and Japanese with Filipinos up to 21%; fully one-fifth would be post-1970 immigrants, although this would be much lower for Japanese. The NLS sample also had too few Asian subjects: the total of 182 compares most unfavorably with the 10,000 who had 1971-1972 SAT results.

The NLS tests lack the social significance of the SAT in that society actually uses the latter to screen for managerial, professional, and technical posts. As for content, the NLS-Verbal tests are very like a lower level SAT-V. The reading comprehension demands less evaluation and inference which means a slight drift away from cognitive skills toward school learning. The NLS-Mathematics test is like the SAT-M in requiring nothing beyond 10th grade algebra and geometry but there is less high level problem-solving and more "rule-following." This means a distinct drift toward school learning, larger here than for the verbal tests (D.A. Rock, personal communication, June 9, 1989). However, should these differences count against the NLS tests? Since university admissions are based on both SAT scores and high school grades, perhaps the NLS tests are closer to the operative criteria than SAT scores alone.

The "Differences" in Table 5.4 show that, when matched with Whites for NLS test scores, Asian Americans (65% Chinese or Japanese) scored 6.9 points below Whites for nonverbal IQ, 4.7 points below for verbal IQ, and 5.8 points below for overall IQ. Comparing the NLS tests to the SAT, Asians could match White performance while giving away more IQ points, indeed, they could spot Whites an extra 1.36 points. This is the pattern one would expect if the above analysis of NLS test content, more emphasis on school learning than the SAT particularly for mathematics, is correct. The "Differences" in Table 5.4 are the product of larger than usual Asian IQ deficits. Since Filipinos were 13 IQ points below other pre-1970 Asian groups, the presence of 21% Filipinos takes the sample mean 2.77 points below Asian samples which exclude Filipinos.

GRADUATE TESTS

During their final year at university or after graduation, those who aspire to elite professions generally take one or more of a collection of tests: the Graduate Record Examination (GRE), taken by those who intend postgraduate study in the humanities, social sciences, and natural sciences; the Medical College Admissions Test (MCAT); the Law School Admissions Test (LSAT); and the Graduate Management Admissions Test (GMAT). The MCAT is administered by the American College Testing Program. However, in 1975-1976, the others were all administered by the Educational Testing Service (ETS) and for simplicity's sake, I call them ETS graduate tests and those who took them in that year the ETS candidate group.

Ideally, we would wish scores for a sample of individuals who took both the Scholastic Aptitude Test (SAT) as 12th graders and the ETS tests four years later, so as to see whether Asians gained or lost ground on Whites

TABLE 5.4
Asian and White Americans 1972
Difference Between IQ and National Longitudinal Study (NLS) Test Scores

Nonverbal IQ	NLS-Math	IQ/NLS
Asian[a] deficit	Asian credit[b]	Difference[c]
2.52	(+)4.37	6.89
Verbal IQ	NLS-Verbal[d]	IQ/NLS
Asian deficit	Asian deficit	Difference
6.07	(-)1.35	4.72
Overall IQ	NLS-Average	IQ/NLS
Asian deficit	Asian credit	Difference
4.30	(+)1.51	5.81

[a]Asians were approximately 34% Japanese, 31% Chinese, 21% Filipino, and 14% other, mainly Korean and Asian Indian. [b]Values for Asian credit (mean above White) or deficit (mean below White) on the NLS tests are analogous to IQ scores, that is, the White *SD* has been put at 15; a NLS credit must be added to an IQ deficit because it shows that Asians were above Whites on the NLS despite lower IQ; a NLS deficit must be subtracted from an IQ deficit because it shows Asians were below Whites on the NLS as well as for IQ (though not as far below). [c]Difference shows how many IQ points Asians fall below Whites when the two groups are matched for NLS scores. [d]The NLS-Verbal score averages two tests, the NLS-Vocabulary and the NLS-Reading.

For key values and calculations, see text.

between their senior year of high school and their senior year of university. That is impossible but as a second best, the ETS candidate group of 1975-1976 is a reasonable match for the postgraduate aspirants from among the SAT candidate group of 1971-1972. There are two complications, Asian immigrants who arrived in the early 1970s and foreign Asians who come to America to do undergraduate degrees, primarily in the sciences and engineering. Fortunately, the GRE results are for U.S. citizens only, which eliminates both groups, since very few post-1970 immigrants would have received citizenship by 1975-1976. The other test results include noncitizens most of whom would be recent immigrants rather than foreign students. Based on MCAT data (Hsia, 1988, pp. 140-141), no test would have more than 20% noncitizens among its candidates, which implies 12% as the upper limit for the total ETS candidate group. Only these 12% should be considered unrepresentative of the earlier SAT candidate group.

Hsia (1983, pp. 133 and 135; 1988, pp. 47 and 51) provided results for all four graduate tests, the GRE and LSAT of 1975-1976, the MCAT of 1974-1975, and the GMAT of 1980-1981. The fact that the MCAT results are a year early for our purpose is trivial, but the GMAT poses a problem. Although from a later era, the GMAT results show Asians doing significantly worse vis-à-vis Whites than on other tests, so to omit it might inflate Asian performance. I decided to present two sets of results: one that applies strictly to those tested circa 1975-1976 and omits the GMAT; one that includes GMAT results with the scores from 1980-1981 being assigned to the candidates of 1975-1976 (Hillhouse, personal communication, June 16, 1989). Given the relative stability of Asian vis-à-vis White performance during the late 1970s, I suspect that the estimates which include the GMAT are the more reliable.

Table 5.5 takes advantage of two things: the fact that the ETS candidate group of 1975-1976 can be considered representative of the graduate aspirants of the SAT candidate group of 1971-1972; the fact that the GRE, MCAT, and LSAT results show Asians above Whites on quantitative tests to exactly the same degree they are below Whites on verbal tests. The latter means that as far as overall test results are concerned, we need not search for a population *SD* for these three tests. All of them are scored on much the same kind of scale and varying values for the population *SD* would merely mean that whatever Asians gained or lost from their quantitative advantage would be balanced out by losses or gains from their verbal disadvantage. The fact the Asian ETS candidates attained parity of overall performance with the white ETS candidates would remain.

Asians were 1.31 points (White *SD* = 15) below Whites on the SAT. By the time they took the ETS tests, Asians had made up that deficit, if GMAT results are not taken into account. And since Asians were 4.45 IQ points below Whites when matched for performance on the SAT, they would be 5.76 IQ points below when matched for performance on the ETS tests (4.45 + 1.31 = 5.76). However, what appears to be a trend over time may be largely due to omitting the GMAT results. As the calculation at the bottom of Table 5.5 shows, when GMAT results are included, parity with Whites on the ETS tests changes into a one-point deficit. This is only marginally less than the Asian deficit on the SAT four years earlier. Therefore, the Asian/White IQ difference probably remained much the same from the SAT to the ETS tests: when matched for performance with Whites on those tests, Asians went from being 4.45 IQ points below Whites to 4.73 points below.

This estimate, that Asians could spot Whites roughly 5 IQ points and match them on ETS tests, rests on a certain assumption. It is assumed that since the ETS candidates were the "survivors" from the SAT candidates of four years before, there was no differential selection for IQ between Asian

TABLE 5.5

Asian and White Americans

Comparison Between IQ/SAT Difference (1971–1972) and IQ/ETS Difference (1975–1976)

Data from ETS graduate tests[a]

	GRE	MCAT	LSAT	Weighted averages
	Asian score minus White score			
Quantitative	+28	+25	–	+27
Verbal	–23	–32	–36	–27
	Number of candidates			Totals
Asian	2 573	1 212	829	4 614
White	178 313	34 672	66 994	279 979

Comparison of differences

	SAT/ETS Asian gain[b]	IQ/SAT difference[c]	IQ/ETS difference[d]
Without GMAT	1.31	4.45	5.76
With GMAT	0.28	4.45	4.73

[a]ETS = Educational Testing Service; names of tests, GRE = Graduate Record Examination, MCAT = Medical College Admissions Test, LSAT = Law School Admissions Test, GMAT = Graduate Management Admissions Test. [b]How much Asians gained on Whites between the SAT (1971–1972) and the ETS graduate tests (1975–1976) measured in points analogous to IQ points (White SD = 15)—see calculation below. [c]From Table 5.3. [d]Difference shows how many IQ points Asians fall below Whites when the two groups are matched for performance on all ETS graduate tests collectively; the values may apply to the group IQ thresholds rather than the means—see text.

Calculation of Asian gains from SAT to ETS:

I.   Without the GMAT results: (1) Asians matched Whites on the ETS graduate tests; (2) Asians were 1.31 points below Whites on the SAT—from Table 5.3; (3) Therefore, Asian gain from SAT to ETS was **1.31** points.

II.   With the GMAT results: (1) Asians (N = 2,132) may have scored 3.56 points below Whites (N = 102,159) on the GMAT, based on 1980–1981 results; (2) GMAT candidates were about 29% of the total candidate group on all ETS graduate tests; (3) When included in a weighted average, the GMAT results put Asians 1.03 points below Whites on all ETS tests (3.56 x .29 = 1.03); (4) Therefore, the Asian gain from SAT to ETS is reduced to .28 points: 1.31 (SAT deficit) – 1.03 (ETS deficit) = **.28** as Asian gain.

and White candidates over that period. Neither group was more highly selected in one sense, that is, as measured by the proportion of its SAT candidates who survived to later take the ETS tests. The ratio of Whites to Asians was 57 to 1 for the SAT candidate group, 56 to 1 for the ETS candidate group. While this makes the assumption stated plausible, it does not put it beyond question. ETS candidates are more elite than SAT candidates and, moreover, Asians have a larger IQ variance than Whites. If the ETS candidates of both groups had a mean IQ the same number of *SDs* above the SAT candidates of both groups, Asians would have reduced their IQ deficit vis-à-vis Whites by almost 2 points. That would imply that when equated with Whites for ETS test performance, the Asian mean IQ would be only 3 points below White rather than 5 points.

On the other hand, the ETS candidate group has an impressively high mean IQ, about halfway between the mean for elite professions and the mean for the less exclusive category of all managerial, professional, and technical posts. If they are elite enough to be considered representative of those who will eventually fill high status occupations, we are less interested in Asian/White IQ differences at the mean than at the threshold. And even if Asian ETS candidates did benefit from differential selection at the mean, the IQ threshold of the Asian group would be at least 5 points below the White threshold. This is mainly due to the mathematics of a normal curve: as Jensen (1980, p. 93, Table 4.3) showed, the threshold difference between two groups is always greater than the mean difference created by those thresholds. This effect is slightly enhanced by larger variance for Asian IQ.

The data suggest these conclusions. When Asians from the SAT candidate group of 1971-1972 took the ETS graduate tests of 1975-1976, they did not lose ground on Whites and may even have reduced their deficit a bit. As for the IQ "Difference" that separates Asians and Whites when matched for performance on ETS graduate tests, the Asian candidates were probably at least 5 points below Whites when IQ thresholds are compared, less than that when IQ means are compared.

UNIVERSITY ENTRANCE AND GRADES

Thus far, we have compared the IQ scores of Asian and White Americans with their scores on various tests of academic achievement. In some cases, the tests lack social significance (Table 5.2) and in other cases, the candidates' IQ scores have been estimated from posited population means (Tables 5.3, 5.4, and 5.5). The ideal data would be university entrance results giving the IQ thresholds of Chinese, Japanese, and Whites admitted to the same university. If the Chinese and Japanese entrants had lower thresholds, we would simply **know** that these groups can meet the same socially significant academic criteria as Whites, despite lower IQs.

TABLE 5.6

Entering Class, University of California, Berkeley, 1966

Estimated IQ Differences between Ethnic Groups at Mean and Threshold

Groups		IQ differences[a]	
		Verbal	Overall
White (–) Chinese[b]	Mean	7.85	4.49
	Threshold	9.57	7.04
White (–) Japanese[b]	Mean	5.04	1.43
	Threshold	5.88	3.02

[a]The IQ differences show how many IQ points Chinese or Japanese entrants fell below White entrants. [b]White (–) Chinese or White (–) Japanese represents White IQ minus Chinese or Japanese IQ.

Example of calculations, difference between White and Chinese thresholds for overall IQ:

(1) From Table 3.2, average of 115.15 (sample verbal mean) and 121.88 (sample nonverbal mean) = 118.515 as sample overall mean; (2) 118.515 – 98.48 (population mean) = 20.035 as gap between sample and population; (3) 20.035 ÷ 16.74 (population SD) = 1.197 as that gap in $SDUs$; (4) Top 28.31% of a normal curve has a mean 1.197 $SDUs$ above its population; (5) Top 28.31% has a threshold .5736 $SDUs$ above its population mean; (6) .5736 x 16.74 (population SD) = 9.60 as that gap in IQ points; (7) 9.60 + 98.48 (population mean) = 108.08 as Chinese IQ threshold; (8) White IQ threshold, calculated by same method with 123 as sample mean from Table 3.2, is 115.12; (9) 115.12 – 108.08 = **7.04** as difference between White and Chinese thresholds.

The only university entrance data in the literature was analyzed in the section on Asian IQ. I refer to the results from Sue and Kirk; (1973) for 210 American-born Chinese, 99 American-born Japanese, and approximately 2340 Whites who entered the University of California at Berkeley in 1966 (see Table 3.2). The fact that these samples shed little light on general population IQs for various groups does not, of course, detract from their value in the present context. The year 1966 puts them before the influx of post-1968 immigrants, the fact that the Asian subjects were American-born avoids the complication posed by foreign and often elite Asians who come to study at American universities.

Table 5.6 shows that Chinese and Japanese Americans who matched Whites in terms of entrance criteria at Berkeley had lower IQ thresholds. The thresholds are the significant comparisons because they represent the minimum IQ members of each group needed to gain entry. The Chinese minimum was 9.6 points below Whites for verbal IQ, 7 points below for overall IQ. The Japanese were 5.9 points below Whites for verbal IQ, 3 points below for overall IQ. The IQ values leave much to be desired - see Table 3.2 and the accompanying text. The verbal IQs are from the SCAT verbal test and sound enough; but the nonverbal IQs are estimates derived on the assumption that the entrants of each ethnic group were as highly selected for nonverbal as for verbal IQ. Therefore, the overall IQs are simply an average of SCAT verbal results and a derivative of those results. The threshold values were calculated using the mean IQs and the mathematics of a normal curve, as described at the bottom of the Table; the threshold differences are larger than differences at the mean for reasons already discussed.

The Berkeley Chinese/White difference of 7 IQ points and Japanese/White difference of 3 points average at 5 points, very close to the values derived from other data. However, before assuming the agreement is real, another factor must be taken into account. Recall the tendency of Chinese and Japanese to perform better vis-à-vis Whites on achievement tests as those tests veered away from cognitive skills and toward school-taught subjects. Therefore, we would anticipate that when Chinese are matched with Whites on highly cognitive tests like the SAT, they would outscore Whites in terms of high school grades. That is exactly the result given by the National Longitudinal Study (NLS). Rock, Ekstrom, Goetz, Hilton, and Pollack (1985, pp. 36-39, Tables 5-1 to 5-4) showed that the Asian 12th graders of 1972 were the equivalent of 1.51 IQ points above Whites on the NLS verbal and mathematics tests (see Table 5.4); and the equivalent of 3.75 points above Whites for high school grades; which gives a cognitive test/grades difference of 2.24 points. In other words, when Chinese plus Japanese and Whites who apply for university entrance are matched for IQ, they should not only outscore Whites by 4.45 points on the SAT (see Table 5.3). They should also outscore Whites by an **extra** margin for high school grades. The total IQ/grades difference would be 6.69 points, that is, 4.45 from the SAT plus 2.24 extra.

Berkeley selects its students using a mix of SAT scores and high school grades and relies upon the latter at least as much as the former. If the weighting were even, the distance between the Chinese plus Japanese IQ threshold and the White threshold should equal the average of their IQ/SAT difference and their IQ/grades difference: $4.45 + 6.69 = 11.14$; $11.14 \div 2 = 5.57$ points. The predicted difference is slightly higher than the 5 points of the Berkeley estimate but, given the limitations of the data, the match is surprisingly good.

What is needed is full data from a number of universities for American-born Chinese, American-born Japanese, and White entrants: comprehensive IQ distributions which make the thresholds clear; SAT scores and high school grades for Asians and Whites matched for IQ. Acceptance for entry must be strictly on merit because otherwise, threshold differences will be blurred by quotas that force Asians to meet more demanding entrance criteria. Such data would do more to partition the factors of Chinese and Japanese overachievement than all data now existent.

ACADEMIC SUCCESS AND FAILURE

Popular accounts of Asian American achievement feature success stories, that is, disproportionate numbers of Asians entering elite professions or elite universities like Berkeley. This can give the impression that Chinese and Japanese Americans outperform Whites primarily at high IQ levels. Moreover, while the mean IQ of Chinese and Japanese is below the White mean, their IQ variance is greater and this means they would match or exceed the percentage of Whites at high IQ levels; for example, all three groups would have 16% of their population above an IQ of 115. This might give the impression that greater variance plays some role, even if a minor one, in explaining Chinese and Japanese overachievement. In fact, Chinese and Japanese Americans outperform Whites at every IQ level and greater variance should hurt as much as it helps. Just as it boosts the number of Chinese and Japanese at high IQ levels, it increases their number at low levels: they would have double the number of Whites below an IQ of 70, that is, 4.5% as compared to 2.3%.

When analyzing the disproportionate number of Chinese and Japanese in elite professions, their greater IQ variance was always taken into account. Therefore, the conclusions reached about high achievers need not be qualified. The analysis of the disproportionate number in the professional, managerial, and technical category proves overachievement at the level of the average person because, at least beginning with the Coleman Report cohorts, 55% of Chinese and 46% of Japanese entered those occupations. And since the IQ thresholds posited for those occupations are close to the population mean, greater variance at that point is simply not a significant factor. However, it remains to show that Chinese and Japanese Americans outperform Whites when the least successful members of each group are compared and this brings us to academic failure.

Census data exist for two criteria of academic failure, although in both cases the values for Whites must be adjusted to eliminate Hispanics. The 1960 census supplies the first criterion: the percentage of Chinese plus Japanese and the percentage of Whites who were scholastically retarded, that is, were enrolled in a grade at least one year below the modal grade for their age. For example, students aged 16.5 years who were in the 10th grade rather than the 11th would be one year retarded, those in the 9th grade two years retarded. The percentage of scholastically retarded rises even in high school, so I used the data for those aged 16 to 17 years (Coleman et al., 1966a, p. 452, Table 6.1.8). The 1980 census supplies the second criterion: the percentage of those who had not yet graduated from high school by ages 25 to 29 (Gardner et al., 1985, p. 25, Table 9). In 1968, these subjects were aged 13 to 17 years, so they provide a good measure of how many students from that era never received their high school diploma. The data do not distinguish those resident in America in the 1960s from post-1968 arrivals but this can be done adequately. For Whites, recent arrivals were so few as to make no difference; for Japanese, they were just over 20% and elite, so rounding their percentage of nongraduates up a fraction gives a good estimate; for Chinese, they were numerous and nonelite and to get a reasonable estimate, I assumed that the 1960s pattern of 2% fewer Chinese than Japanese persisting to the 12th grade is a reliable guide.

As usual, to compare Chinese plus Japanese against Whites, we want White IQ thresholds, this time for those Whites who avoid academic failure. And once again, these can be calculated given the percentage of Whites above the threshold and the correlation between IQ and the relevant kind of academic achievement. For scholastic retardation, 88.1% of Whites avoided that fate and I used a correlation of .65, which is the correlation between IQ and learning to read (Jensen, 1980, p. 325). For failing to graduate, 88.6% of Whites avoided that and I used a correlation of .58, which is the correlation between IQ and amount of education for adults (Jensen, 1980, p. 334). These values dictate 78 as the White threshold for avoiding scholastic retardation, 76.6 as the IQ threshold for avoiding nongraduation. Once these are established, the values for Chinese plus Japanese mean IQ and *SD* give estimates for the percentage of that group we would expect to fall below the thresholds, **if** they behaved like a White subgroup. And the actual percentage who are scholastically retarded or fail to graduate will tell us how differently they actually do behave from a White subgroup.

The first estimated percentage in Table 5.7 shows that 18.5% of a White subgroup, analogous to Chinese plus Japanese for IQ profile, would be scholastically retarded. In fact, only 6.9% of Chinese plus Japanese fall behind their age cohort, a remarkable IQ/achievement gap. If the total gap were due to a lower IQ threshold, the Chinese plus Japanese value would be an IQ of 63.5, which is so far down into the range of mental retardation as to seem absurd. Therefore, I assumed, without evidence, that Chinese plus Japanese must have a higher capitalization rate than Whites, indeed, that only half as many fail to capitalize on their ability to keep up with their age cohort. Even this puts their IQ threshold at 70, 8 points below White, and means that only the mentally retarded lacked the capacity to keep up. The second

TABLE 5.7
Chinese and Japanese Americans Compared to White Americans: IQ and Academic Failure

| Group | Percent | | IQ | Capitalization |
	Estimated[a]	Actual	Threshold[b]	rate
Scholastically retarded[c]				
Chinese & Japanese	18.5	6.9	70.1	97.5%
White	–	11.9	78.0	94.8%
Nongraduates[d]				
Chinese & Japanese	18.4	5.0	69.2	99.0%
White	–	11.4	76.6	94.2%

[a]Estimated refers to the percentage of Chinese and Japanese who would have been either scholastically retarded or without a high school diploma, if this were determined purely by their population IQ mean (98.48) and *SD* (16.74) as compared to Whites. [b]The threshold gives an IQ above which either the scholastically nonretarded or graduates would score; the values for Chinese and Japanese thresholds are speculative and based on the assumed capitalization rates—see text. [c]The scholastically retarded are those who, in 1960, were aged 16–17 years and were at least one grade behind for their age. [d]Nongraduates are those who were aged 13–17 years in 1968 and had not yet graduated from high school when aged 25–29 years in 1980.

estimated percentage in Table 5.7 shows that 18.4% of a White subgroup, like Chinese plus Japanese for IQ, would be nongraduates. In fact, only 5.0% of Chinese plus Japanese fail to graduate, an even more striking IQ/achievement gap. If that total gap were due to a lower IQ threshold, the Chinese plus Japanese value would be an infinite number of *SDs* below the White threshold, which is logically absurd. Therefore, I put their capitalization rate at a virtual maximum, assumed that 99% of them capitalize on their ability to graduate. This puts their IQ threshold at 69, which is about 7.5 points below Whites, and one point below the criterion of mental retardation.

The comments about mental retardation should not be taken literally. What the data really show is that if IQ tests are used to classify Chinese and Japanese Americans as mentally retarded, they lose all contact with reality. At least in the 1960s, in terms of any real world criterion of mental retardation, everyone above that level simply was not capable of graduating from high school. The data also confirm our generalization about the extent to which Chinese and Japanese Americans outperform Whites. They outperform Whites at every IQ level, indeed they may do even better at the bottom of the curve that at the top; and lower IQ thresholds and higher capitalizations rates play their part at every level. The only surprise is that low IQ Japanese probably outperform low IQ Chinese.

THE CLASS OF 1966

The achievements of the postwar generation of Chinese and Japanese Americans have been detailed one by one, but they can also be presented as a continuous narrative. The story of that generation is really the story of the Chinese and Japanese who graduated from American high schools in the mid to late 1960s. I will call them the class of 1966.

They were born circa 1948 and raised in homes roughly equivalent to Whites in terms of socioeconomic status. The Chinese members were 65% American born and 35% foreign born, the Japanese 89% and 11%. In 1980, 14 years after graduation, the Chinese American and foreign born did not differ significantly for achievement as measured by occupational status, the Japanese American-born did slightly better.

In grade school, the class of 1966 had lower verbal IQs than Whites and no higher nonverbal IQs, although they were more precocious on tests of map skills and figure copying. When matched with Whites for IQ, they outperformed them on achievement tests by a small margin, equivalent to about 2 IQ points, doing better in English than mathematics, particularly well in spelling. Very few of them were scholastically retarded and this persisted into high school. Only 6.9% ever lagged a grade or more behind their age group as compared to 11.9% of Whites.

By high school, their overperformance on achievement tests had become highly significant, equivalent to about 5 IQ points, and the balance between subjects had altered. When matched for nonverbal IQ, they outperformed Whites on mathematics tests by 6 points; when matched for verbal IQ, they outperformed Whites on English tests by 3 or 4 points. Their over-performance was higher on tests of school-taught subjects than cognitive tests and highest of all in advanced mathematics, indeed, tests of analytic geometry and calculus showed huge overperformances of up to 15 points. When matched with Whites for IQ, they did better in terms of high school grades than on the typical achievement test, overperforming by the equivalent of almost 7 IQ points. Few dropped out of high school and some of these later returned to earn their diploma. Eventually 95% would graduate as compared to just under 89% of Whites.

During their senior year of high school, the Coleman Report confirmed that the class of 1966 had lower IQs than their White counterparts: a nonverbal IQ of 100, a verbal IQ of 97, an overall IQ of 98.5. During their junior and senior years, at least 50% took the Scholastic Aptitude Test (SAT) while the figure for Whites was less than 30%. This 5 to 3 ratio was very close to that they would later achieve in attaining high status occupations. Despite being much less highly selected than White SAT candidates, they were only 1.31 points below Whites overall, being slightly superior on the SAT-mathematics, suffering from a deficit on the SAT-verbal. They could concede 4.5 IQ points and yet match Whites for SAT scores, concede almost 7 points and match Whites for high school grades. This meant they could gain entry to the same universities as Whites despite lower IQs. At Berkeley in the fall of 1966, American-born Chinese entrants had an IQ threshold 7 points below Whites, American-born Japanese a threshold 3 points below.

They were as successful at university as Whites: their final year found them contemplating graduate study with a per capita advantage over Whites equal to the 5 to 3 ratio they had enjoyed when contemplating undergraduate study. On the Graduate Record Examination (GRE) and admissions tests for medical, law, and business schools, they either matched or bettered their performance of four years earlier. Indeed, between the SAT and these graduate tests, their small SAT score deficit vis-à-vis Whites was probably reduced to one point or less.

In 1980, when 32 years of age, the Chinese members of the class of 1966 had 55% of their number in managerial, professional, or technical occupations, the Japanese 46%, their White contemporaries only 34%. This meant that Chinese Americans had mimicked a subgroup of the White population with a mean IQ of almost 120 which was 21 points above their actual mean; and that Japanese had mimicked a White subgroup with an IQ of 109 which was 10 points above their actual mean. In 1980, the Chinese members of the class had incomes $2,000 above their White contemporaries, the Japanese $1,700 above.

The explanation of these massive IQ/occupational achievement gaps lay in certain ethnic differences. Chinese Americans could qualify for high status occupations with an IQ threshold about 7 points below the White threshold, which gave them a pool of potential achievers larger than their mean IQ would have led one to expect. Japanese Americans had an IQ threshold about 3 points below the White threshold. Moreover, the class of 1966 capitalized on its available pool of talent with extraordinary efficiency: 78% of its Chinese members who were capable of entering professional, managerial, or technical occupations actually did so; 74% of its Japanese members did so. Whites capitalized on only 60% of their available pool of talent. This ends our account of the class of 1966.

HYPOTHESES AND EVIDENCE

Two hypotheses have dominated our account of Chinese and Japanese American overachievement, namely, the hypotheses of lower IQ thresholds and higher capitalization rates. Only the former can be directly evidenced and it can now be summarized as can the evidence in its favor. The threshold hypothesis asserts: that Chinese and Japanese outperform Whites when matched with them for IQ; and conversely, that Chinese and Japanese secure entry into the same universities and high status professions as Whites despite lower IQ. Table 5.8 rehearses the evidence for these assertions, tries to match that evidence to the chronology of the class of 1966, and partitions Chinese and Japanese overachievement into a threshold factor and a capitalization rate factor.

In Table 5.8, the "ideal years" refer to the chronology of the passage of the class of 1966 through grade school, high school, and university. The "actual years" refer to when the evidence relevant to their overachievement vis-à-vis Whites was actually gathered. The actual does not always correspond to the ideal, but the match is better than might appear. The evidence for achievement tests in grade school is a decade late, but still before the influx of post-1968 immigrants began to alter the composition of the older Chinese and Japanese communities. The match between actual and ideal years for miscellaneous tests taken in high school is excellent. The actual year for SAT data is 6 years late, but recall that the candidate group was 99% pre-1970 and about 80% Chinese and Japanese. The ETS graduate test data are from the appropriate year given the date of the SAT data. The university entrance results are a perfect match for the ideal year.

From entry into high school through graduation from university, Table 5.8 shows great consistency. There are five estimates of how far the IQ threshold of Chinese plus Japanese falls below the White threshold, when they are matched with Whites for academic achievement. These vary within the narrow range of 4.45 to 5.81 points and average at 4.94 points. Unfortunately, the university entrance results are from one university only and are the sole piece of data that differentiates Chinese from Japanese for the threshold factor. Those results have been used to partition the IQ/occupational achievement gaps: the Chinese gap for the class of 1966 was 21 IQ points, which divides into 14 points from a higher capitalization rate and 7 from lower IQ thresholds; the 10-point Japanese gap divides into 7 points from the capitalization factor and 3 from the threshold factor.

This summary of the evidence points in two directions at once. On one level, the evidence that Chinese and Japanese overachievement can be partitioned into two factors is overwhelming. Indeed, without something

TABLE 5.8

Class of 1966

Factors of Overachievement, Chinese and Japanese Americans, Born Circa 1948

Academic achievement

		Year[b]		Distance below white threshold[c]		
Achievement measure[a]	Grade	Ideal	Actual	Chinese	Japanese	Both
Stanford Achievement Tests	4–6	1957–60	1968	–	–	2.24
Miscellaneous Tests	9–12	1962–66	1960–70	–	–	4.68
Scholastic Aptitude Test	12	1965–66	1971–72	–	–	4.45
National Longitudinal Study	12	1965–66	1972	–	–	5.81
University entrance	13	1966	1966	7.04	3.02	5.03
ETS graduate tests	16	1969–70	1975–76	–	–	4.73

Occupational achievement

				Factors[d]		
Achievement measure	Group	Age	Year	IQ Threshold	Capitalization rate	IQ/achievement gap[e]
Managerial, professional	Chinese	32	1980	7.00	14.00	21.00
& technical occupations	Japanese	32	1980	3.00	7.00	10.00

[a]In descending order, for detail and results, see Tables 5.2 (Grade school—Berkeley only), 5.2 (High school—All studies), 5.3, 5.4, 5.6, and 5.5. [b]The ideal year is that in which these cohorts should have been tested to match their grade level; the actual year is that in which relevant samples were tested. [c]How far the IQ threshold for Chinese or Japanese or both was below the White IQ threshold, when they and Whites were matched for achievement; sometimes the values are based on mean rather than threshold differences—see relevant tables and text. [d]The factors partition the Chinese and Japanese IQ/occupational achievement gaps into: the number of IQ points due to a lower threshold for entry into the occupations named; the number due to a higher capitalization rate—see Table 5.1, note a. [e]From Table 4.4.

like the threshold and capitalization factors, the phenomenon would be simply inexplicable. On another level, the evidence is too weak to determine the exact magnitude of the factors posited or the balance between them. The next chapter develops and extends this theme, that is, it assesses the status of most of what we have learned about Chinese and Japanese Americans and attempts to distinguish the probable from the tentative.

6

The Probable
and the Tentative

Cromwell, addressing the Long Parliament, gave good advice when he said: "I beseech you in the bowels of Christ to consider whether or not you may be mistaken." Before drawing implications, prudence dictates a review of our key estimates and distinctions. These include estimates of the mean IQs of Chinese and Japanese Americans, the classification of tests as IQ or achievement, estimates of the IQ/occupational achievement gaps, and partitioning those gaps into threshold and capitalization factors.

POPULATION MEAN IQS

Here I feel a tension between truth and dialectic. The fact that so many studies require adjustment is bound to arouse skepticism and it would have been good tactics to err on the side of higher values for the mean IQ of Chinese and Japanese Americans. But in doing this, there is the danger of not telling the truth as you see it. I have tried to adjust all studies as fairly as possible. However, I now want to show that alternative adjustments would not in fact push values much higher and answer points raised by various critics. The best format is to divide the literature into the Coleman Report and a collection of all studies other than the Coleman Report.

Other Studies

In Table 3.10, nine studies were described as having some degree of reliability and these put the mean IQ of Chinese and Japanese Americans at about 97. I can see no case for alternative adjustments of the more reliable of these studies, namely, Berkeley (1968), Kauai (1965-1966), Wyoming (1943-1945), and Project Talent. There are elements of uncertainty, the 33.5 years of obsolescence at Kauai, the high nonresponse rate in the Project Talent follow-up, but no one has suggested an alternative reading that would better deal with these problems. Several points have been made concerning the remaining studies, some more plausible than others.

The best suggestion concerned the Ethnic Minorities Research Project: the results from the one Chinese private school, rather than being simply omitted, could be included by being given a weight of 9.92%, which was the percentage of Chinese school children attending private schools at that time. This would raise the value for Chinese plus Japanese IQ from the Ethnic Project by one point. It was suggested that the results from Chinatown (1972) and Chinatown (1975) be merged, on the grounds that the sample size of the former was so small that the divergence between the two might be due to chance. Moreover, that the adjustments for Chinatown (1975) were too complex: why not just assume the comparison group of Bakersfield Whites was representative and simply norm the Chinese children against them, adjusting only for 5.5 years of obsolescence? I believe that Chinatown (1972) and Chinatown (1975) differ not because of chance, but because of the influx of post-1968 immigrants, and that norming against Bakersfield Whites inflates verbal IQ. But here, I am following the policy of accommodating all suggestions to note the lack of effect.

No one has actually suggested treating the Whites of Hawaii (1960-1963) and Los Angeles (1969-1970) as representative, but let us adopt the fiction that they were. For the Stewart et al. study of Hawaiian Chinese and Japanese, this means scoring them against the White members of the Caucasian sample. Therefore, let us simply deduct the Puerto Ricans and Portuguese from the sample, thereby ignoring the doubts Vernon (1982, p. 95) expressed about the whole sample and the census data which reinforced those doubts. For the Project Access study of Orientals in Los Angeles, it means scoring them against the almost nonexistent sample of inner-city Whites, thereby ignoring the warnings Flaughter (personal communication, August 13, 1987) gave about casual samples and the evidence that middle-class Whites had abandoned the area far more than other groups.

TABLE 6.1
Selected Studies from Table 4.1 with Some Values Revised

Results of studies

Study	Year	N	Status[a]	IQ[b] Nonverbal	Verbal	Overall
Berkeley	1968	234	2	98	95	96
Kauai	1965–1966	253	2	99	97	98
Wyoming	1943–1945	669	2	–	96	–
Project Talent	1960	150	2	97	96	96
Chinatown	1972–1975	307	2/3	102(1)	96(7)	99(4)
Hawaii	1960–1963	554	3	–	99(3)	–
Los Angeles	1969–1970	390	3	107(8)	103(8)	105(8)
Ethnic Project	1950–1969	1018	3	–	–	99(1)

Estimates of mean IQ

Studies	Basis of estimate	IQ Nonverbal	Verbal	Overall
Status 2–3	Weighted average	101.63	97.73	99.40
Status 2–3	Median	100.00	96.67	98.33
Coleman Report	Grade 12 only	100.25	96.70	98.48

[a]Key to status categories—see Table 4.1; [b]Numbers in brackets show the result of each revision, that is, how many points the revised value adds to the original value.

Table 6.1 lists the nine studies relevant to our estimate of the mean IQ of Chinese and Japanese Americans. Four of them have been revised in accord with the suggestions discussed and Table 6.1 allows us to note the effects. Where results have been revised, the new value is accompanied by a number in brackets: these show how many points were added to the original values and range from 1 to 8 points. Taking the weighted average of all these studies, Chinese and Japanese Americans now have 101 plus for nonverbal, 98 for verbal, and 99 plus for overall IQ. The weighted average gives great weight to the extreme results from the least reliable sample of all, inner city Los Angeles. Therefore, median values were calculated as well, and these give 100 for nonverbal, 96 plus for verbal, and 98 for overall IQ. The suggested adjustments have simply raised values to approximate those we have used throughout, partially so as to err on the side of caution. They give no support to Chinese or Japanese superiority.

Gordon and the Coleman Report

Robert A. Gordon of Johns Hopkins (personal communication, October 23, 1989) posed a question concerning the estimates of Oriental IQ from the Coleman Report. He noted that they were based on scoring Orientals against Whites who were in the same school grade, for example, Oriental 12th graders were scored against White 12th graders. If the former were younger than the latter within each grade, would that not lower Oriental performance and deflate their mean IQ? In reply, age-within-grade differences do exist but have no real significance.

First, the age-within-grade differences that separate Orientals and Whites are very small. The Coleman Report does not give the average age of its samples but does give scholastic retardation data from the 1960 census (Coleman et al., 1966a, p. 452, Table 6.1.8). When about 3% Hispanics are removed from Whites, we can compare the percentage of Orientals and Whites enrolled in a grade below the modal grade for their age. Census data show that a group's average age within a grade is almost entirely a function of its scholastic retardation percentage and therefore, we can estimate the relevant age differences. Oriental children averaged about .03 years younger than White children at the 3rd grade level and this rose to about .10 years younger at the 12th grade level, that is, Oriental 12th graders were 17.4 years of age and Whites 17.5 years.

Second, age-within-grade differences have a very limited effect on test performance. The SCAT verbal was used as the verbal IQ test in the Coleman Report. Data comparing those in a given grade to those one grade below show the younger subjects with an IQ deficit of 12 points at the 3rd grade level, much smaller deficits at the 6th and 9th grades, a deficit of only 2.4 points at the 12th grade level (Educational Testing Service, 1957, Tables H1-H9). Data from Raven and Court (1989, p. 8) show nonverbal tests giving an IQ deficit of 10 points at grade 3, which falls away to no more than 2 points at grade 12. But all of these are age-**plus**-grade effects, not age-**within**-grade effects, and the former give an exaggerated impression of the latter. In other words, the younger subjects in the SCAT and Raven's tables suffered not only from being a year younger but also from being a grade lower. Since their scores were deflated by having had less schooling, they do not measure the impact of age-within-grade differences, where all subjects have had the same amount of schooling. Recently, de Lemos (1989) and McDonald (1989) succeeded in isolating age-within-grade differences and showed that these have absolutely no effect on performance on group verbal tests. Even more surprising, de Lemos found only minimal effects on a nonverbal test, namely, Raven's Standard Progressive Matrices.

This implies that the age differences between the Orientals and Whites of the Coleman Report had no effect on verbal scores and negligible effect on nonverbal scores. Concerning the latter, even if half of the age-plus-grade effect were assigned to age-within-grade, Orientals would lose no more than two-tenths of a point at any grade level. At the 12th grade, they would lose one-tenth of a point: if an age-within-grade difference of a full year costs one point (half of 2 points), the fact they were younger by one-tenth of a year cost them one-tenth of a point. No doubt, there are other small biases in the Coleman Report data, for example, Orientals may have had their scores inflated by a tenth of a point because a greater percentage of Whites were in private schools. But these things are hardly worth an adjustment.

Lynn and the Coleman Report

Lynn (in press) attacked the Coleman Report on two grounds. First, he contended that the nonverbal tests used "were tests of math ability largely set out in verbal format and this will have given the tests a verbal bias and handicapped Orientals." Therefore, he questioned whether these tests were a good measure of general intelligence or g and noted that Coleman himself took care to state they were not measures of intelligence.

I can only assume that Lynn confused the Coleman Report's mathematics achievement test with its nonverbal test. As Jensen (1980, pp. 478 & 481) pointed out, the nonverbal test given to grades 6 to 12 features figural classification (particularly oddity problems) and nonverbal analogies "highly typical of ... group IQ tests used in schools"; and in commenting on the predictive validity of the tests, Jensen noted that the nonverbal test is primarily a measure of g alone, whereas the verbal test loads on both g and a verbal ability factor. At least half of the Coleman Report's nonverbal test closely resembles Cattell's Culture Fair Test of g . The items load very heavily on fluid g and qualify as highly culturally reduced, the kind of items often given to illiterates or foreign language speakers. Jensen considered oddity problems so culturally reduced that he used them to rank various species, such as nonprimates, the lower primates, monkeys, apes, and human children, for intelligence (Jensen, 1980, pp. 132, 155-156, 178-179, 229, & 234).

As for Coleman refusing to call his tests measures of intelligence, I too have my doubts about IQ tests as measures of intelligence. However, that has nothing to do with the fact that if anything is to be called a nonverbal IQ test or a measure of psychometric g, the Coleman Report's nonverbal tests must be so called. Of course, I have no objection to the Coleman Report's mathematics achievement tests being described as having a verbal component that handicapped Orientals. Rather than being unfriendly to our analysis, that would help solve a problem we have examined at some length: why Chinese and Japanese subjects did not overperform on the Coleman Report's mathematics achievement test, as compared to their mean IQ.

The second problem Lynn posed concerns the fact that the school children tested by the Coleman Report classified themselves as to ethnicity. He noted that if all Filipinos classified themselves as "Oriental", they would constitute 20% of the Coleman Report's Oriental sample and only the remaining 80% would be Chinese and Japanese. The three studies existent (see Table 7.1) suggest 85.3 as the mean IQ of Filipino Americans circa 1965 and while this is a tentative estimate, the true value was probably at least below 90. Therefore, a Filipino presence would pull down the mean IQ of the Oriental category and make that value an underestimate of an undiluted sample of Chinese and Japanese.

The possibility of a Filipino presence was noted in our discussion of the Coleman Report but Lynn's assertions call for a more detailed treatment. It is important to get an exact calculation of its possible effect and, as far as the Coleman Report 12th graders are concerned, this is given at the bottom of this page. It shows that if all Filipinos classified themselves as "Oriental" in 1965, they would have constituted 19.23% of the Coleman report 12th graders. Note that by the 12th grade, about 20% of Filipino Americans had dropped out of school, which compares to a White attrition rate of 15% and would lift their mean IQ from 85.3 to 86 (see Table 2.3). The calculation shows that a total Filipino presence would imply a mean IQ for Chinese and Japanese of 101. Similar calculations show that 55% of all Filipino 12th graders would have to classify themselves as "Oriental" to get the Chinese/Japanese 12th grade mean to 100. Taking the Coleman Report sample that embraces all grades from 3 to 12, even a total Filipino presence would give a Chinese/Japanese value of only 99.6. A 60% Filipino presence would give 98.5, the value we have assumed throughout.

Coleman Report - effect of **all** Filipinos present in the 12th grade sample: (1) Assume 7.5% attrition for Chinese and Japanese, 20% attrition for Filipinos, and deduct 0.5% of Filipinos as ethnic Chinese, which gives Filipinos as 19.23% of the Oriental 12th graders in 1965 (Bureau of the Census, 1960, PC(2)-1C, Tables 3, 4, & 5; 1970, PC(2)-1G, Tables 3, 18, & 33; Coleman et al., 1966a, p. 450, Table 6.1.3); (2) Put IQs of 12th graders at Filipino = 86, Oriental unadjusted = 97.6; (3) Solve for Chinese/Japanese unadjusted IQ, $86 (19.23) + x (80.77) = 97.6 (100)$, which gives 100.36; (4) Adjusted for Chinese/Japanese attrition less than White (see Table 2.3), $100.36 + .88 = \textbf{101.24}$.

As to the question of whether Filipinos would actually classify themselves as "Oriental", I wrote Mayeske who was chief author of all the follow-up studies of the Coleman Report data and he consulted his colleague Okada, the coauthor who was expert on Asian Americans. His reply (Mayeske, personal communication, October 8, 1987) is worth quoting at some length: "My colleague Okada says that he doubts that Filipinos would classify themselves as Oriental rather than Other back in 1965 but given the opportunity they would classify themselves as Asians. He cautions that not everyone that we would classify as Filipino is physically homogeneous. For example, a very Oriental looking person from the Phillipines might classify themselves as such because of their appearance whereas a Mexican looking Filipino would probably never classify themselves as Oriental. In working with the Coleman data we always assumed that there were probably some Filipinos in the Oriental sample but that their incidence was very small.".

To estimate the size of the "very small" number who would identify as Oriental, I wrote the Population Division of the US Bureau of the Census. The only Filipinos of Oriental appearance or origin were those of Chinese ethnicity. N.R. McKenny (personal communication, October 16, 1987) who is Assistant Division Chief, Ethnic and Racial Statistics Program Areas put the number at less than 0.5% of all Filipino immigrants. She also noted that the census abandoned the term "Oriental" and adopted "Asian" as the classification for Filipinos after "we discussed the issue with representatives of the Filipino community in the US." As a further check, I wrote Jensen who responded (personal communication, September 15, 1987) after approaching a leading member of the California Filipino community: "...who said that she had never known a Filipino who would categorize his or her ethnic membership as Oriental; if it were a choice between 'Oriental' and 'Other,' they would always pick 'Other.' However, if the multiple-choice options included 'Asian,' most Filipinos would pick that category, assuming the category of 'Filipino' was not available". Bell (1985, p. 24) added to the consensus when he noted that in 1965, the term "Oriental-American" applied to Asian Americans of Chinese and Japanese origin.

Lynn's critique of the Coleman Report omitted the fact that there is a totally independent body of evidence concerning the mean IQ of Chinese and Japanese Americans in which Chinese and Japanese subjects are unambiguously identified. I refer to the nine studies in Table 4.2 which compares the mean IQs of Chinese and Japanese Americans and puts both at approximately 97.6. Lynn did note that some studies other than the Coleman Report used the term "Oriental": these are Berkeley 1968, Project Talent, and Los Angeles 1969-1970. Jensen (personal communication, August 27, 1987) assured me that in his Berkeley study, only Chinese and Japanese were classified as "Oriental" and that Filipinos were classified as "Other".

Project Talent does not appear in Table 4.2 so its sampling is irrelevant. Let us alter the Table in two ways: following Lynn, discard Los Angeles because of its use of the term Oriental; and using the generous adjustments made earlier in the chapter, revise the values of the Chinatown studies and Hawaii 1960-1963 upward (see Table 6.1). All of this would do no more than raise the Table 4.2 estimates of Chinese and Japanese IQ to 98.5, the value we have assumed throughout.

In sum, to get the mean IQ of Chinese and Japanese Americans even one point above Whites at 101, we must assume the following: that all other studies should be discarded in favor of the Coleman Report, including those which identify Chinese and Japanese subjects unambiguously; that the total data of the Coleman Report should be discarded in favor of sole reliance on its 12th graders; that most Filipinos classify themselves as Orientals. None of these assumptions seem plausible *ad seriatim* and the package as a whole goes well beyond the boundaries of the probable. I conclude that all probable estimates must be 100 or less and believe that 98.5 is the most judicious estimate, recognizing that the nature of the data precludes any exact value from being more than tentative. This estimate applies of course only to the post-war generation of Chinese and Japanese Americans.

THE CLASSIFICATION OF TESTS

Mental tests have been classified as IQ or achievement tests. Other critics might take an opposite tack from Lynn. For example, they might call tests like the SCAT-Quantitative, or even the SAT-Mathematical and NLS-Mathematical, nonverbal IQ tests and use them to demonstrate Chinese and Japanese superiority. However, labels do not alter reality. This kind of classification would merely mean that these groups show clear superiority only when nonverbal IQ is measured by mathematical items. The tests I have called nonverbal use letter groups and shapes that pose oddity problems, figure classification and analogies, pictorial classification and logical relationships, picture completion and arrangement, spatial analogies, figure and number series, mazes plus line-and-dot mazes, block design and object assembly. The data do not preclude the possibility that Chinese and Japanese excel on some of these, but they show no advantage over Whites on the total package. It is difficult to avoid the conclusion that Chinese and Japanese outscore Whites for "nonverbal IQ" only when the term becomes a synonym for "mathematical achievement". Classifying achievement tests in terms of their degree of school loading is another matter and poses many problems. It underlines the need for direct evidence of a performance gap between IQ tests and socially significant academic achievement, that is, between IQ and SAT scores and school grades.

IQ/OCCUPATIONAL ACHIEVEMENT GAPS

The best estimates give gaps of 20 points for Chinese and 10 points for Japanese respectively. These were calculated by comparing the actual mean IQ of the Coleman Report cohorts with the much higher values we would estimate based on their occupational achievements. Since the actual mean might be off by a point or so, and since occupational IQ thresholds introduce an ambiguity in the estimated values, the true gaps could be anywhere between 15 and 25 points for Chinese, anywhere between 5 and 15 points for Japanese. It is most improbable that the Chinese gap is less than 15 points, that is, less than one White *SD*.

THE THRESHOLD AND CAPITALIZATION FACTORS

I have put the Chinese IQ threshold for high status occupations at 7 points below the White IQ threshold. Therefore, if the Chinese IQ/occupational achievement gap is 20 points, it divides into 7 points from the threshold factor, the remaining 13 points from more efficient capitalization upon those who can qualify for high status occupations. The 10-point Japanese gap divides into 3 points from the threshold factor and 7 points from the capitalization factor. The estimates of the threshold factor are highly tentative. They do not cover those who create a managerial role for themselves through personal initiative, as distinct from academic credentials, but these are not numerous enough to matter much. The main problem is the character of the academic achievement data. Only one study differentiates Chinese and Japanese and although five studies give consistent values for Chinese plus Japanese, most of them suffer from a serious weakness. They give only achievement test scores for Asians and Whites, leaving us to calculate candidate IQ scores based on population mean IQs. If Asian population means are closer to White than assumed, Asian candidate IQ would be closer to White candidate IQ and Asian IQ thresholds closer to the White threshold.

Therefore, if our estimates of population mean IQs were a bit low, that would have several consequences. As already described, it would affect the size of the Chinese and Japanese IQ/occupational achievement gaps. But it would also affect the threshold factor and thus alter the relative potency of the threshold and capitalization factors in explaining those gaps. For example, assume that our estimate of Chinese population mean IQ was 1.5 points too low and the true mean was 100. Then the Chinese IQ/occupational achievement gap falls from 20 points to 18.5; the threshold factor falls from 7 points to 5.5; and because the capitalization factor is simply whatever remains, it would stay at 13 points. Clearly the balance would shift in favor of the capitalization factor over the threshold factor. The former would outweigh the latter by 2.36 to 1 (13 ÷ 5.5) rather than 1.86 to 1 (13 ÷ 7).

THE LIMITS OF THE TENTATIVE

The tentative status of the exact values for population mean IQs has limited significance. Altered values would affect the balance between the threshold and capitalization factors. However, they would not put the Chinese or Japanese mean above the White mean and they would not challenge the existence of huge Chinese and large Japanese IQ/occupational achievement gaps. At long last, we can state the implications of our analysis and ask the new questions that arise whenever old questions are answered. When doing this, I use my best estimates throughout, but the reader should feel free to substitute more conservative values. None of the implications will be much affected.

7

Beyond Genes and IQ

The fact that Chinese and Japanese Americans have a slightly lower mean IQ than Whites, or at least no higher IQ, and yet outperform them academically and occupationally can be approached in two ways. First, as a discovery with profound implications for ethnic, gender, and national groups. Second, as a phenomenon that both calls out for explanation and poses the more general problem of what factors actually determine the achievements of ethnic groups in America. The implications gradually merge into the causal problem and therefore, we begin with them.

IQ AND SINO-JAPANESE GENES

Theories about the genetic superiority of the Sino-Japanese peoples for intelligence are now suspect, no matter what evolutionary scenario is proposed. Japanese in Japan and Chinese in China, although here the evidence is mainly from overseas Chinese, may have a 1- to 5-point advantage in terms of overall IQ over White Americans. But that advantage disappears when all three groups are raised in a more uniform environment, that is, the environment of postwar America.

Japanese in Japan open up a 14-point gap between nonverbal and verbal IQ when scored against White Americans. But after they have been in America a generation or two, even that huge gap at least tends to disappear. In 1938, when Chinese and Japanese Americans were still largely unacculturated, Honolulu gave these results: Chinese children went from a 12-point nonverbal/verbal gap at ages 10 to 12 down to a 5-point gap at ages 13 to 14; Japanese children went from a 20-point gap down to 13.5 points (see Table 2.1). It may be said that even the older children showed a significant difference but that was to erode over the next generation. By 1965, the Coleman Report showed all ages with only a 3.62-point difference between nonverbal and verbal IQ and the oldest subjects with only 3.55 points (see Tables 2.3 and 4.1). The ancestors of the Coleman Report 12th graders would have included some White and Hawaiian admixture but rough calculations based on intermarriage rates put this at only 10% to 20%. Therefore, subjects with entirely Chinese or Japanese ancestry would show a gap of about 4.2 points ($3.55 \div .85 = 4.19$). On the other side of the ledger, recall that 19% of the cohort were foreign born and can hardly have been fully acculturated. It is of interest that the nonverbal/verbal gap expands again when a new wave of immigrants arrive, for example, note the 12-point difference in Chinatown in 1975 (see Table 3.8).

Nonetheless, I suspect that one factor of the nonverbal/verbal gap may have a genetic basis. Nonverbal tests differ in the extent to which they contain items most demanding in terms of spatial visualization, visualizing the outcome of rotating figures in space, disembedding target figures from a larger pattern. On tests with a heavy emphasis on such items, Chinese and Japanese Americans may have an advantage that will prove resistant to acculturation. Nagoshi and Johnson (1987) partialled out the contribution general ability or g makes to mental test performance, leaving residual spatial and verbal factors. They found that, compared to Hawaiian whites, Hawaiian Japanese had a large spatial/verbal gap which held even for the offspring of American born parents.

The significance of this difference between Japanese and Whites, whether genetic or not, is not great. These residual factors are well removed from real-world problem solving. For example, as the next section shows, groups with poor performance on spatial visualization subtests have outstanding records even in areas like mathematics. And note that residual factors are not measures of functional abilities. Even when a subject takes a spatial subtest, his or her general ability makes an important contribution and when that is partialled out, what is left is an abstraction that does not function independently. If Lynn is correct in his evolutionary scenario, which shows Sino-Japanese developing visuospatial ability at the cost of lower verbal ability, that development may be one history has rendered counterproductive.

The fact a specialized visuospatial ability conferred survival advantage during the ice ages does not mean that it confers an achievement advantage in a modern industrial society.

In sum, Chinese and Japanese do not seem to have any genetic superiority for overall IQ and probably have no genetic superiority for any specialized ability that confers an overall advantage in terms of group achievement.

Those favoring a hypothesis of Sino-Japanese superiority are left with three options. First, they can suggest that Chinese and Japanese suffer from some disadvantage within the American environment. To do this, they will have to accept the very same challenge they laid down for environmentalists, that is, find something that affects IQ other than the text-book factors of SES and quality of home environment. As we have seen, the postwar generation of Chinese and Japanese Americans were raised in homes that matched Whites for SES and other indexes of environmental quality. The possibility that they suffered from some unknown handicap cannot be dismissed, but the hypothesis remains untestable until the relevant factors are identified and that is not going to be easy (Flynn, 1987b).

Second, they can suggest that selective migration brought to American shores an inferior sample of Chinese and Japanese. Lynn (in press) took this option. He argued that a majority of Chinese and Japanese Americans were descended from early immigrants, that those early immigrants came to work as unskilled laborers, and that such work may have attracted those of below average ability. Fortunately, Vernon (1982, p.37) has done his usual excellent survey of the literature on Japanese Americans. In 1969, Glazer referred to them as originating in peasant stock but all later scholars fall into two groups: Strong and Sowell who concluded that Japanese immigrants were above average with overrepresentation of the middle class; Petersen and Kitano who concluded that all classes were represented with only later arrivals superior. None of these four endorsed overall inferiority.

As for Chinese Americans, a detailed account of the literature appears later in this chapter. For now, a few comments. The early immigrants were from peasant stock but Lynn is simply mistaken when he says a majority of Chinese Americans are descended from them. Focusing on the post-war generation, no more than 20% of their ancestors arrived before the Chinese Exclusion Act of 1882 and these came from a China of which 80% to 90% were peasant farmers and villagers. That Act was designed to eliminate peasants and workers in favor of merchants and scholars. It hardly did that but it did eliminate the least successful who could not raise the $1,000 needed to qualify. Many still came to do menial jobs but that did not show a lack of ambition, quite the contrary. Thousands upon thousands made desperate efforts to get to America, despite interment and hardship and persecution, hoping to amass the capital that would upgrade their status, at first in China and later in America. Nothing suggests that Chinese immigrants were either superior or inferior to Chinese in general. We also have a piece of indirect evidence, namely, that Chinese and Japanese Americans have virtually the same mean IQ (see Table 4.2). If the Japanese were not negatively selected, the Chinese can hardly have been, unless one puts forth the ad hoc hypothesis that Chinese are superior to Japanese for IQ.

Third, those who argue for Sino-Japanese superiority over Whites can attack IQ tests: they can hypothesize that the tests cannot compare Asian and White Americans for intelligence because of the cultural distance that separates them. But this totally undermines the international data on which the claim of genetic superiority rests: if IQ tests cannot bridge the cultural distance between Chinese, Japanese, and Whites all of whom are American born, what of the greater cultural distance that separates Chinese in China, Japanese in Japan, and Whites in America? A variation on this third option may seem more promising: concede that IQ tests cannot compare Asian and White populations for intelligence, but suggest that their respective achievements can do so, and that therefore Asians are more intelligent. That is certainly an open option but much must be done before it is operational. We would have to develop a theory of achievement so robust as to suggest a criterion that could, in a nonpartisan way, rank peoples across cultures. And since no one would argue that intelligence alone dictates achievement, it would have to be detailed enough to separate out all the factors that influence a people's achievements.

No one has a mortgage on the future but for the moment, the burden of proof has shifted away from environmentalists and toward those who hold theories about the genetic superiority of the Sino-Japanese for intelligence. That said, we turn away from issues such as whether IQ measures intelligence to confront a more limited question: no matter what it measures, what limits does the mean IQ of a group set on its potential achievements?

IQ AND GROUP ACHIEVEMENT

Non-IQ factors often overwhelm mean IQ as determinants of group achievement. They can do this because of their great potency and their capacity to operate independently of IQ. If we ignore the role of non-IQ factors, we risk setting too strict limits on the potential achievements of certain groups, for example, the potential of low-IQ ethnic groups to solve their economic and social problems, the potential of women to achieve in mathematics, and America's ability to compete successfully with Japan.

The Potency of Non-IQ Factors

Non-IQ factors such as whatever causes lower IQ thresholds and higher capitalization rates differ between ethnic groups, and sometimes have the same potency as 20 points added to a group's mean IQ. This is implicit in what has gone before but its derivation can be made explicit. If Chinese Americans had no ethnic differences from Whites, they would need 20 points added to their mean IQ to attain their occupational achievements. Thanks to lower IQ thresholds and higher capitalization rates, they attain their occupational achievements with no IQ points added. Therefore, those factors have the same potency as 20 points added to their mean IQ. The ethnic differences that separate Japanese and White Americans have the potency of 10 IQ points.

The Independence of Non-IQ Factors

A familiar formulation of factors that contribute to achievement runs IQ + motivation + opportunity = achievement (Jensen, 1980, p. 241). For the moment, let motivation stand for all non-IQ factors productive of achievement, a more complex analysis to be suggested later. Motivation may be a potent factor in addition to IQ, but its practical importance would be undermined if it operated simply as a dependent variable. Assume that motivation differences between groups were always positively correlated with IQ differences between groups: motivation would then merely enhance the advantage of the higher IQ group and do nothing to limit the effect of mean IQ on group achievement. Jensen (1973, pp. 246-247; 1986, pp. 450-451) argued that this is the case not only within groups but also between groups, or at least between Black and White. He hypothesized that high-IQ children enjoy success and gain motivation, whereas low-IQ children are discouraged by failure and lose motivation.

Motivation may be dependent on IQ within groups but it operates independently between groups. We have already seen some obvious examples: Chinese Americans are much more motivated than Whites despite lower or at least no higher IQ, more motivated than Japanese despite the same IQ; Japanese Americans are more motivated than Whites despite no higher IQ. More examples are to come: Filipino Americans are much more motivated than Whites despite lower IQ, perhaps more motivated than Japanese despite lower IQ; Jewish Americans are far more motivated than non-Jewish Whites, at least toward mathematics, despite lower visuospatial

IQ. Non-IQ factors do not simply follow in the train of IQ but can have a powerful countervailing effect.

The Mismeasure of Group Potential

Over the last few years, Jensen (1973), Gottfredson (1987), and Nichols (1987, p. 215) have all emphasized the potency of the mean IQ of ethnic groups in determining their real-world achievements. Nichols went the furthest: he argued that the IQ deficit of Blacks means nothing can be done to reduce deficits in occupation, income, family demoralization, and crime.

Jensen used the Black IQ distribution to account for the underrepresentation of Blacks in professional, technical, and white-collar occupations, the dearth of Blacks who can qualify for America's better universities, the overrepresentation of Blacks among those classified as mentally retarded. However, it is important to note that Jensen never said "nothing can be done" and advocated a variety of educational and social reforms. Gottfredson used the mean IQ and variance of Blacks to explain their underrepresentation among physicians, engineers, teachers, and a variety of middle status occupations, but her data do not show actual Black/White ratios that correspond to those predicted. Rather, as she noted, her data show ratios that correspond to those predicted on the assumption that Black IQ thresholds for certain occupation are 7.5 points lower than White thresholds. I would add that the data could as easily be explained by hypothesizing that Blacks have higher capitalization rates.

These scholars all qualified their thesis. However, they tended to place less emphasis on the qualifications than on the thesis itself: witness Gottfredson (1987, p. 510) and her assertion that "occupations themselves can be viewed as analogous to differentially g - loaded mental tests." Chinese and Japanese Americans help us appreciate the extent to which ethnic groups are **not** simply the captives of their IQ means and variances. Thanks to potent ethnic differences operating independently between groups, Chinese and Japanese Americans have opened up huge IQ/achievement gaps. It may be said that their example has little applicability to other groups. After all, their mean IQ is 98.5, while Hispanics have a mean of 86 and Blacks a mean of 85. Perhaps there is a critical level below which non-IQ factors cannot operate independently but must follow in the train of IQ. In reply, the fact that Chinese and Japanese outperform Whites at every level of the IQ curve, even at the level of mental retardation, casts doubt on this objection. But there is another ethnic group, quite different from Chinese and Japanese in culture and evolutionary origin, whose record of achievement reinforces our doubts.

TABLE 7.1
Filipino and White Americans 1979: IQ and Economic Status

IQ studies

Study	Year	N	Age (years)	IQ
Hawaii	1960–1963	79	15–17	83
Kauai	1965–1966	138	9–10	91
Western City	1977=1971[a]	46	25	82

Average IQ: 85.3 or 85.8 normed on Whites inclusive of 4% Hispanics.

IQ and economic status

Group	IQ	High status[b] occupations	Income[c]	Families above poverty level
White[d]	100.0	27.0%	$15 572	93.0%
Filipino[e]	85.8	29.3%	$14 664	93.8%

[a]Subjects tested in 1977 but most resident in America before 1971. [b]Percentage of each group who held managerial, professional, and technical posts in 1980. [c]Median income of full-time workers, aged 15 years and over, in 1979. [d]Whites inclusive of 4% Hispanics. [e]Filipinos from 1980 census who were resident in America pre-1970.

Filipinos and Whites

Table 7.1 uses the three studies existent to estimate the mean IQ of Filipino Americans resident in America prior to 1970 at 85.3. It then uses the 1980 census to show that these Filipinos matched Whites for economic status, that is, they surpassed Whites for occupational status, had 94% of White income, and had fewer families below the poverty level. All IQ and economic data have been adjusted just as they were for other Asian groups. (Bureau of the Census, 1980, PC80-1-C1, Tables 125, 163, & 164; East-West Center, undated, Table 7, pp. 1729-1744, and Table 11, pp. 330-331; Gardner et al., 1985, p. 34, Table 14).

There is indirect evidence that Filipino occupational achievement follows the Chinese pattern. If one assumes the same values for IQ variance, IQ thresholds, and capitalization rates, the predicted percentage in high status occupations is close to the actual percentage. On the other hand, it should be emphasized that no firm conclusions can be drawn until the post-war generation of Filipino Americans has been thoroughly researched. The IQ studies are weak and I suspect that the true value for pre-1970 Filipino IQ was closer to 90 than 85. Also achievement was uneven within the pre-1970 Filipino community, women outperformed men and post-war immigrants outperformed native-born males, so we need a better match between IQ data and achievement data. At present, all we can say is that this group looks promising as an example of overachievement by a group whose mean IQ falls below the White mean. Note that Filipino Americans have benefited from positive selective migration over the last two decades (Gardner et al., 1985, p. 25) and today's population may well enjoy higher IQs and levels of achievement than the pre-1970 population.

It would be wrong to suggest that other groups will necessarily imitate Chinese or Filipinos. Black Americans are showing an alarming tendency to divide along class lines. The lower half are losing ground and yet, at the same time, some powerful force is pushing the upper half beyond the putative limits of mean IQ. The ratio of White to Black in managerial, professional, and technical occupations should be 3.15 to 1. In 1980, the actual percentages of Whites and Blacks in those occupations were 27% and 16.8% respectively, a ratio of 1.61 to 1 (Bureau of the Census, 1980, PC80-1-C1, Table 125). Blacks were achieving high status occupations at double the number their mean IQ would dictate. The phenomenon is welcome but understanding requires discrimination between the roles of IQ thresholds and capitalization rates and on a practical level, between "affirmative action" programs that are beneficial and those that are counterproductive.

This emphasis on exceptions to the accuracy of mean IQ as a predictor of occupational achievement could give a false impression. I do not deny that mean IQ is often an excellent predictor of a group's achievements. My point refers to potential rather than actual achievement and is causal rather than predictive: even when mean IQ predicts the actual achievements of a certain group, it lacks the causal potency to determine that group's potential achievement; on the other hand, even though non-IQ factors have the potency to enhance a group's real-world performance, they may never in fact operate to do so.

Jewish Americans and Women

It might appear that mean IQ mismeasures the potential achievements of only ethnic groups. Therefore, it is worth noting one case that serves as a bridge between ethnicity and gender. The fact that women tend to be underrepresented in mathematics and science has attracted considerable attention. Fox (1976) showed that far more males than females have exceptional mathematical ability; Maccoby and Jacklin (1973) showed that males tend to do better on tests of spatial visualization. Jensen (1980, p. 626) hypothesized that the two are related: that visuospatial IQ is a potent mediator of mathematical ability and that therefore, sex differences there account for the mathematical superiority of males. Against this hypothesis, there is an ethnic group whose mathematical achievements provide a striking counterexample.

Table 7.2 gives results for Jewish subjects normed on non-Jewish Whites of the same sex. The Project Talent results (Backman, 1972, p. 5, Table 1) show that Jewish subjects can turn a 10-point deficit for visuospatial IQ (VS-IQ) into a 10-point advantage for mathematical achievement, giving fully 20 points as their VS-IQ/mathematical achievement gap. The mathematics was high school mathematics ranging all the way from decimals to analytic geometry and calculus. The visual reasoning scores were based on 55 items of which 40 required visualizing the outcomes of manipulating figures in two and three dimensional space (Flanagan & Cooley, 1966, p. 79).

As Table 7.2 shows, the pattern of Jewish overperformance in relation to VS-IQ is confirmed elsewhere. Majoribanks (1972) got results for 100 Jewish Canadians and 100 White Anglo-Saxon Protestants, all males 11 years of age, on both the PMA space and PMA number (elementary arithmetic) factors. The Jewish subjects overperformed by 15 IQ points. Lesser, Fifer, and Clark (1965, p. 48) tested 80 Jewish children and 80 Chinese children, ages 6 to 7 years from New York City, on spatial visualization and numerical (basic arithmetic) scales. I scored the Jewish against the Chinese children, equated the Lesser Chinese children with the Project Talent Oriental sample, and thus derived Jewish scores based on the Project Talent non-Jewish White norms. These scores have little credibility but do show that Lesser's results are at least compatible with the Project Talent results.

Table 7.2 also treats the mean VS-IQ of Jewish Americans as an unknown that must be estimated from their occupational achievements. Weyl's data (1969, Tables IV and V) show that Jewish outnumber non-Jewish White Americans as mathematicians and statisticians by a per capita ratio of over 3 to 1. No one knows what VS-IQ threshold holds for White Americans who enter these occupations but Matarazzo's data suggest a value above the elite professions in general, perhaps 112 after adjusting for obsolescence. When Jewish Americans are treated as a subgroup of White Americans in general, these values give them an estimated VS-IQ of 121, which is 30 points above their actual VS/IQ from Project Talent. We cannot factor this huge IQ/occupational achievement gap with much confidence, but the fact that Jewish Americans overperform by 20 points in high school mathematics would give: 20 points from a lower threshold; the remaining 10 points from a higher capitalization rate.

TABLE 7.2
Jewish Visuospatial IQ (VS-IQ) and Mathematical Achievement

Test scores when normed on non-Jewish Whites of same sex[a]

Study	Sex	N	Age (years)	Math	VS-IQ	Difference
Project Talent	M	658	17	111	90	21
Project Talent	F	578	17	110	91	19
Project Talent	M/F	1236	17	111	91	20
Majoribanks	M	100	11	112	97	15
Lesser et al.	M/F	80	6–7	113	92	21

VS-IQ estimated on basis of occupation and actual VS-IQ

Occupation	Threshold[b]	Ratio[c]	Estimated[d]	Actual[e]	Difference
			VS-IQ		
Mathematician	112	3.46	121	91	30
Statistician	112	3.44	121	91	30

[a]The Jewish subjects from Majoribanks were normed on White Anglo-Saxon Protestants; the Jewish subjects from Lesser et al. were first scored against the Lesser Chinese sample, that sample was equated with the Project Talent Oriental sample, and that gave scores against the Project Talent White norms—see below for example of calculations. [b]The threshold gives an IQ above which about 90% of each occupation would score. [c]The ratio is the per capita ratio of Jewish to White Americans in each occupation. [d]Estimated VS-IQ refers to means for Jewish Americans in general calculated from the thresholds and ratios—see Table 4.3 for example of calculations. [e]Actual VS-IQ is the mean from the Project Talent Jewish sample.

Examples of calculations, Jewish mathematics test score, Lesser et al.:

(1) Jewish mean on Number Scale = 28.50, Chinese mean = 27.79; (2) 28.50 − 27.79 = .71, that + 9.35 (Chinese SD) = .076 SDU; (3) Chinese mean and SD set at 100 and 15; (4) .076 x 15 = 1.14, that + 100 = 101.14 as Jewish mean normed against Lesser Chinese; (5) Project Talent Oriental mean for mathematics = 111.65 (Table 2.4) or 11.65 points above Project Talent non-Jewish Whites; (6) 101.14 + 11.65 = 112.79 or **113** as Lesser Jewish mean, scored against Project Talent non-Jewish Whites.

Lynn (personal communication, August 9, 1990) and Gordon (personal communication, October 23, 1989) objected that the Jewish VS-IQ/mathematical achievement gap can be explained by other factors in their ability profile. Jewish Americans have a higher verbal IQ than non-Jewish

Whites, perhaps a higher overall IQ, and the thesis is that general reasoning processes, expressed verbally, can often solve mathematical problems. In other words, they believe that a more sophisticated IQ measure, based on averaging visuospatial and verbal scores or even placing primary emphasize on verbal IQ, can explain mathematical achievement when Jewish ethnicity and gender are combined.

Table 7.3 uses the Project Talent data (Backman, 1972, p. 5, Table 1) to falsify that hypothesis. It explores all possible combinations created by Jewish ethnicity and gender, that is, pairs Jewish males with non-Jewish White females, and so forth. It also gives the mathematical achievement differences that remain when such groups are equated on various IQ measures. In so doing, it shows that every gain from calling on verbal IQ to mitigate the failure of visuospatial IQ is lost somewhere else. For the sake of completeness, Table 7.3 compares sole reliance on visuospatial IQ, with a score that averages VS-IQ and verbal IQ so as to give them equal weight, with sole reliance on verbal IQ. As we go along the continuum from visuospatial to verbal, it is true that the mathematical achievement difference between Jewish and non-Jewish Whites drops, at least when gender is held constant: for example, the difference between Jewish and non-Jewish White males falls from 21 points to 1 point. However, following that same continuum expands the mathematical achievement difference between the sexes, when ethnicity is held constant: for example, the difference between Jewish males and Jewish females rises from 17 points to 27 points.

When ethnicity and gender distinctions both come into play, the pattern becomes highly eccentric. Matching Jewish females and non-Jewish White males for visuospatial IQ leaves a mathematical achievement difference of only 4 points. But matching Jewish males and non-Jewish White females leaves 37 points and moving toward verbal IQ shows the members of both pairs separated by huge gaps of 26 to 30 points. However, rather than being distracted by detail, the thing to note is how badly all the IQ measures do when applied over all six of the combinations created by ethnicity and gender. Moving along the IQ continuum generates average differences which hardly change at all, that is, vary only from 18.3 to 19.3 points. Which is to say, manipulate the IQ data as you will, when Jewish ethnicity and gender are combined, no IQ measure comes close to explaining differences in mathematical achievement. The potency of non-IQ factors is at least 1.22 standard deviations ($18.3 \div 15 = 1.22$). Until these factors are taken into account, we have no real explanation of the fact that American females do not at present match the mathematical achievements of American males.

TABLE 7.3

Project Talent: Jewish and Non-Jewish Whites, Male and Female
Score Differences between Various IQ Measures and Mathematical Achievement

Groups	IQ measure		
	Visuospatial[a]	VS/Verbal[c]	Verbal[b]
Jewish male & non-Jewish White male	21	11	1
Jewish female & non-Jewish White female	19	11	3
Jewish male & Jewish female	17	22	27
Non-Jewish White male & non-Jewish White female	16	22	29
Jewish female & non-Jewish White male	4	11	26
Jewish male & non-Jewish White female	37	33	30
Average score difference between IQ and math[d]	19.0	18.3	19.3

[a]Differences between Visuospatial IQ and mathematical achievement are based on VIS and MAT factor scores from Project Talent. [b]Differences between Verbal IQ and mathematical achievement are based on VKN and MAT factor scores. [c]VS/Verbal IQ gives equal weight to both Visuospatial and Verbal IQ; the differences between this measure and mathematical achievement are not always the average of the Visuospatial and Verbal differences because of the use of absolute values. [d]The average score differences, and all others, are calculated in terms of White *SDs* with the value set at 15.

America and Japan

The fact that Japan may have an IQ advantage over America has struck some scholars as a fact of great significance. They have hailed it as the key to understanding both the actual and potential achievements of those two nations. Lynn (1987a, p. 465) asserted that the Japanese advantage played a significant role in that country's economic miracle because it "takes brains to drive Western industrialists out of their own markets." Basiuk (1984), writing in *Foreign Policy,* perhaps the most influential policy-making journal in the English language, sounded a note of despair: international power has become a function of human resources rather than natural resources; and Japan's human material is simply so much better than that available in the United States. Rushton (1989, p. 12) included the Chinese in his prognosis. The future of world history has been determined because "the Oriental populations of the Pacific Rim must be expected to . . . outdistance the predominantly Caucasian population of North America and Western Europe."

This kind of concern is misdirected. Rather than worrying about the 1 to 5-point IQ advantage Japan or China might have, we should be worrying about the non-IQ advantage of 11 to 20 points American-born Japanese and American-born Chinese enjoy over Whites. If such an advantage exists when cultural differences are blurred within the United States, by shared language, schooling, and media content, it may be at least as great when cultural differences are at full strength, between peoples still in their respective countries of origin. Stevenson et al. (1985) supplied one piece of evidence that such is the case. They showed that at least in three comparable cities, Japanese schoolchildren in Japan and Chinese schoolchildren in Taiwan have roughly the same IQs as White Americans but open up huge nonverbal IQ/mathematics gaps. Indeed, as early as the 5th grade, they open up the kind of gap Chinese and Japanese Americans do not achieve until advanced mathematics courses in high school (see Tables 2.4 and 5.2). When normed on White Americans, Japan's 5th graders had a 19-point gap between nonverbal IQ (as measured by Coding and Spatial Relations) and school-taught arithmetic, Taiwan's 5th graders a 16-point gap. Clearly non-IQ factors give Japan and Taiwan a far greater pool of those who can qualify to play scientific and technological roles. Whether they better capitalize on their available pool of talent, whether they actually outperform America in terms of scientific creativity and technological achievement, that poses a truly difficult problem of measurement. The fact that both have enjoyed economic miracles may be relevant but hardly decides the question.

Given that the overachievement of Chinese Americans is double that of Japanese Americans, it may seem tempting to speculate that mainland China is poised on the brink of its own economic miracle. After all, the Chinese appear to have potent non-IQ factors no one else can match. However, once again I must emphasize that the fact non-IQ factors realize their potential in one cultural setting does not guarantee they will do so in another. Just because the combination of Chinese IQ and non-IQ factors proves adequate to outcompete White Americans for high status occupations does not mean it is adequate to solving China's economic, political, and demographic problems. That may be a much more formidable task, solved many generations hence or not at all. When we say that Chinese possess non-IQ factors worth 20 IQ points that quantity has not been measured on an absolute scale. It is norm referenced, the norms being supplied by the performance of White Americans on IQ tests and the American occupational ladder.

Even Japan's economic miracle, which has actually occurred, is not fully understood. It is best to stick to what we know. First, wherever Japan outperforms America, IQ plays a marginal role. Second, if Japan has better human material, it is because some non-IQ facet of Japanese culture is both advantageous and based on a genetic difference. No one knows whether this last is true and therefore, no one knows whether its competitive advantage is permanent. World history affords many surprises and American influence may wax rather than wane, something which may or may not be a reason for optimism.

EXPLAINING GROUP ACHIEVEMENT

The non-IQ factors that influence group achievement cannot really be lumped together under the rubric of "motivation": that was merely a short-hand device. What progress has been made in identifying non-IQ factors, and how successfully can they explain the most spectacular case of overachievement, namely, that of Chinese Americans? A whole literature on this subject created by historians and social scientists is conspicuous by its absence from the works of psychologists. It is as if it were dammed up behind an intellectual barrier: I suspect that barrier is constructed out of overemphasis on mean IQ and if so, the dam should be broken and a stream of ideas allowed to flow through.

The Author Seeks Rapport

To exploit this literature, certain inhibitions must be set aside. Whenever ethnic groups are compared, some offense may be given; for example, if Irish are said to have a less potent work ethic than Chinese Americans, or Black families said to be less educationally efficient than White families. As an Irish American with a record of activity in the Black protest movement, when such a thing was possible, the author has no desire to promote stereotypes of lazy and drunken Irish, or unmotivated and drug addicted Blacks. Comparative statements about groups do not apply to individuals, of course: variance for traits within groups is always greater than variance between them; the most sober and hard-working person in America could easily be Irish or Black. I have tried to defuse group comparisons by relying primarily on scholars from the ethnic group concerned, Rose Hum Lee and Tan and Wang for Chinese Americans, Moynihan and Woodham-Smith for Irish Americans, Sowell and Staples for Black Americans. Everything said can be checked against the original sources and the reader will often find my language more circumspect than the original.

However, I have not tried to sanitize my account of these groups beyond a certain point. At best, such a thing would mean surrender to that passionate ideal of every journal editor, a dead-stick prose that alienates every reader except the academic. At worst, it means the loss of important insights. Given the tendency to write off inner-city Blacks as hopeless, because of their levels of violence, solo-parent homes, and drug addiction, it is terribly important for Americans to know that other groups eventually made it despite similar statistics of social despair. Kant said "two things above all excite the mind: the starry heavens above and the moral law within". But Kant never had an opportunity to study the differential achievements and histories of American ethnic groups. It is a fascinating story and it must be kept alive. I suggest that offense may be avoided if three ground rules are obeyed: read in common sense qualifications; check original sources; explore whether a negative comparison does not ring true with the ethnic group concerned.

As the above implies, the author has depended heavily on other scholars for data and methodology, particularly Thomas Sowell. Sowell (1975) made brilliant use of the comparative method: he isolated some 15 factors which have influenced the fate of American ethnic groups, historical, sociological, demographic, and contextual factors, as well as psychological. I have adopted a similar method to explain the differential achievements of Chinese Americans as a high achievement group, Irish Americans as an average group, and Black Americans as a low achievement group. Brevity will mean some oversimplification and there are differences between Sowell and myself on questions like the role of government, so he must not be held responsible for what follows.

The Chinese and the Irish

The central causal problem for the Chinese is explaining the achievements of the American born members of the post-war generation, those born shortly after 1945. Their immigrant ancestors were peasants and villagers in the mid-19th century but many participated in the shift to Chinese coastal cities which accelerated as the century progressed. Chinese stranded in America by the collapse of Nationalist China in 1949, plus those who came after that date, had longer urban experience but they are irrelevant. The ancestry of our target group can only be roughly estimated from immigration and fertility data, but a reasonable break-down would be as follows: no more than 20% of their ancestors arrived before 1882; at least 60% arrived between 1882 and 1924; and no more than 20% arrived between 1924 and 1947 (Lee, 1960, pp. 7-41).

Perhaps 5% of Chinese immigrants over this whole period were intellectuals who came to America for university training, although it could have been somewhat less. Virtually all of the remainder came from the Pearl River delta, an area south of Canton with Hong Kong in its mouth. The 19th-century immigrants were laborers and peasants, the Chinese Exclusion Act of 1882 was designed to upgrade them to merchants and students, the Immigration Act of 1924 was meant to stop immigration entirely. After 1882, some continued to come directly from peasant and village China, others spent a generation or so in Canton or Hong Kong. The most and least successful were underrepresented. The most successful never left China or returned home to stay, the least successful could not save or borrow the $1,000 needed to qualify as a "merchant". The students were young boys and teenagers who came to school in America, sometimes only for a year or two in order to gain entry. Throughout the whole period Chinese who were American citizens brought over children born in China and after 1924 these were the main source of immigration. Many of these children were fictitious products of the "slot racket" and insured a fairly random sample of the home village. For example, a Chinese born in America in 1870 had by 1957 brought over 57 of his "sons", who had in turn brought over 250 of their "sons", which is to say he was personally responsible for the entry of almost the entire male population of his village. In 1957, it was estimated that at least half of San Francisco's Chinatown were products of the slot racket or other forms of illegal immigration (Lee, 1960, pp. 78-81, 95, & 302-304; Wang, 1966, pp. 96-98).

The Pearl River delta has been the home of an intense rice-based agriculture for over 4,000 years. The unrelenting work demanded may be greater than any other area in the world. Two rice crops and one dry crop are produced each year, horticulture produces vast quantities of fruit, tea and silk (from mulberry bushes) are marketed, vegetables and sweet potatoes grown, livestock include chickens, pigs, buffaloes, and fish farms. These conditions engendered a powerful work ethic and Chinese immigrants to America have manifested that ethic from the 1850s right up to the present. Every observer has commented on the pace of work, the hours of work, the propensity to save and invest in their children's education (Bodde, 1957, p. 52; Brand, 1987; Butterfield, 1990; Fairbank, Reischaur, & Craig, 1965, pp. 90-91; Lee, 1960, pp. 52, 144-145, & 254-257; Petersen, 1978, p. 75; Tan, 1986, pp. 16-17 & 171-171; Vernon, 1982, pp. 274-275).

Irish immigrants came from a 19th-century rural Ireland in which conditions could not have been more different. Half the rural population lived in mud huts, tilling a quarter to a half-acre, farms only one-sixth the size of those prevalent in China. In order to avoid starvation, these farms were given over almost entirely to the optimum crop, namely, potatoes. Potatoes required little more than spading and turning a few weeks of the year, all improvements were the property of the landlord, and tenants could be turned out at will. Irish peasants spent most of the year in enforced idleness. They were not crushed, travellers remarked on their hospitality, love of music and dance, and gaiety. But no potent work ethic developed. When the Irish came to America, they were often content with a bare sustenance, even this was a welcome relief after famine Ireland. They made a grand thing out of Saturday night, given over to sociability and fighting, and if the best street-fighter on the block died poor, he had moments of glory unknown to a cost accountant. Irish Americans may have lacked a positive attitude toward work but some of them had a very good time. As for the Chinese, Lee noted something that adds a fascinating corollary to our thesis. The Sze Yap people have been less achieving than other Chinese Americans: these people came from the periphery of the Delta where soil was less fertile and agriculture less intense (Glazer & Moynihan, 1970, pp. 238-239, 246, & 259-262; Lee, 1960, pp. 385-386; McAleavy, 1967, p. 31; Woodham-Smith, 1962, pp. 18-37, 268, & 409).

Traditional China gave education an all-pervasive role, indeed, it provided the foundation on which rested the entire political, social, economic, and cultural life of the Chinese people. Confucianism conferred dignity on peasant labor, peasants were ranked second only to the Mandarin class, and the traditional Chinese examination system was the only way a village youth could rise to the Mandarin class. The periodic examinations were great public events and preparation for them so arduous that it led to a virtual examination way of life. Those who passed the first level were called "budding geniuses", those who passed the second "promoted scholars", those who passed the third became high officials, the best often became prime minister and married a royal princess. Those who attained high office were expected to foster the interests of their villages of origin and whole families, clans, and villages pooled their resources to give their brightest boy the leisure to prepare for the exams (Fairbank et al., 1965, pp. 84-88; Hu, 1962, pp. 3 & 13-15; Lee, 1960, pp. 96-97; Menzel, 1963; Wang, 1966, pp. 13-14).

American Chinese from the start emphasized education and looked upon money earned from academic status and professional credentials as more honorable than mere money alone. The Chinese family became one of the most educationally efficient in America, rivalled only by the Japanese and Jews. There was the usual generational strife found in immigrant families, but above the battle certain assumptions were rarely contested. Children were expected to study hard and did so, earning high marks irrespective of IQ, which gave the Chinese unusually low IQ thresholds for entry into high status occupations. The Coleman Report shows Oriental students doing many more hours of homework, having better attendance records and higher aspirations; the National Longitudinal Study adds confirmation, plus showing they spent far less time on athletics and extra-curricular activities. Parents tried to protect their children's time by discouraging part-time jobs. Chinese youths identified their self-esteem with academic advancement, targeted themselves for the best universities, and rarely passed up a chance for professional status when they could qualify, which gave Chinese Americans as a group a high capitalization rate on their available pool of talent. An Irish youth might forfeit a promising opportunity so as to attend a Catholic college, stay with kin or friends, marry the girl or boy next door, a Chinese rarely (Coleman et al., 1966a, p. 24; Hsia, 1988, p. 78; Lee, 1960, pp. 185-230, 374, 382, & 392; Petersen, 1978, pp. 92-93; Rock et al., 1985).

Ireland was the only European country that did not establish a single university during the Middle ages. By the 19th century, the mass of people had no educational tradition of any sort thanks to 130 years of the penal laws which forbade Catholics from attending school, running schools, even sending their children abroad to be educated. Even those few who escaped to Britain and whose children attended college were remarked upon by their contemporaries for their lack of commitment. When Irish immigrants came to America, there was no presumption that families should sacrifice to educate their young. The first objective was ownership of a family home and everyone was expected to contribute: children dropped out of school, sacrificing education and future skills, to work and augment family capital and income. Devout parents discouraged education as a threat to faith. When the Irish rose out of poverty, they did not identify their worth with professional advancement, but sought status as political orators, singers, entertainers, athletes, military heros. For many Irish, the ideal was a secure civil service job and real life was lived outside of work, arguing religion or politics or becoming the best raconteur at the local saloon (Kessler-Harris & Yans-McLaughlin, 1978, pp. 114-120; Glazer & Moynihan, 1970, p. 258; Sowell, 1975, pp. 71-80, 127, 146-147, & 205; Woodham-Smith, 1962, p. 27).

Confucianism also emphasized sobriety and moderation and Chinese Americans have always had low rates of alcoholism. The 19th-century Irish relieved their idleness, and the fact their lives had no overriding private or public purpose, with cheap poteen or illegal whisky and alcoholism became the bane of Irish American immigrants with high rates persisting to the present day. Cross-cultural analogies are chancy. However, the Irish remind one of Ruth Benedict's Native Americans of the plains, Dionysian and given to exuberance, excess, and romantic individualism, among whom alcohol spread like a plague; while the Chinese seem like the Pueblos of the Southwest, Apollonian with a love of harmony, moderation, and order, for whom liquor was no temptation (Benedict, 1946, pp. 79-88; Bodde, 1957, pp. 78-79; Glazer & Moynihan, 1970, pp. 257-258; Hu, 1962, p. 6; Tan, 1986, p. 32; Vernon, 1982, pp. 184-185; Woodham-Smith, 1962, pp. 25 & 268).

By 1945, Chinese Americans had developed enormous potential for achievement and when America finally lowered artificial barriers, the combination of educationally efficient families, targeted professional status, hard work, discipline, and sobriety took the post-war generation straight to the top. Irish progress was painfully slow, as late as 1900 the wild Irish slums were often deemed hopeless. The Irish were noted for violence, street fighting, gang warfare, organized terrorism, the Irish draft riots alone killed ten times as many as all the Black riots of the 1960s; alcoholism was higher than alcoholism plus drug addiction among today's Blacks; as late as 1915, 50% of all Irish families suffered from broken homes. William Dean Howells lamented that the movement of one Irish family into a neighborhood was enough to spread fear and panic as residents abandoned their dwellings and fled (Sowell, 1975, pp. 62, 73-75, 89, & 134).

However, beneath the surface, constructive forces were at work. Nineteenth-century Irish Americans created two great institutions, the political machines of cities like New York and Boston, and the American Catholic Church. They arrived in America fresh from the Catholic emancipation movement, for which purpose Daniel O'Connell had created the first fully fledged, mass-based, political party of the modern world. Drawing on their Irish background, they organized a politics based on corruption and personal reciprocity, which gave them a vast pool of party positions. New York's county committees grew to number 32,000 persons and had to hold their meetings in Madison Square Garden. They gave themselves lucrative patronage, civil service jobs, paving contracts, construction work, jobs on the police force, all of which did much to lift the

Irish out of poverty. To this day, Irish are much overrepresented among municipal workers and in 1958, 54% of Brooklyn Catholics had relatives or close friends on the police force (Glazer & Moynihan, 1970, pp. lxxxiv & 223-228; Sowell, 1975, pp. 79 & 183).

The Irish in Ireland had been devoted to their priests, for their courage when outlawed, their patriotism, and their heroism during the great famine; the Irish in America supported the Catholic Church at great sacrifice. The Church responded with its charities and its schools, whose priests, brothers, and nuns spent themselves in an unrelenting struggle to give Irish the literacy and numeracy that took them to the middle class. Catholicism was not all gain: the Irish participated in a world-wide phenomenon, namely, the failure of Catholic nations and ethnic groups to distinguish themselves in science. Whatever the explanation of that phenomenon, the stock explanation is that Catholics believe they already understand the world, looking for IQ differences between Catholics and Protestants scarcely promises much (Glazer & Moynihan, 1970, p. 231; Sowell, 1975, pp. 75-76; Woodham-Smith, 1962, p. 341).

In 1950, after 80 years on the urban frontier, Irish Americans finally matched Americans in general for economic and social status. They have not gone beyond that, they may be a bit above average for occupational status but they are a bit below average for income (age-adjusted family income). They do not rival the Chinese but the days of "colored man preferred, no Irish need apply" are gone forever (Glazer & Moynihan, 1970, pp. 254 & 324; Sowell, 1975, p. 152, 1978b, p. 21, 1978c, pp. 257-258 & 336-339).

Blacks and the Irish

There are three different groups of Black Americans and, as Sowell pointed out, these groups had very different histories. In 1860, before the Civil War and the abolition of slavery, some Blacks were "free persons of color", a group that had an enormous head-start on other Blacks in terms of self-direction of their lives, skill acquisition, literacy, and urbanization. Today the offspring of these Blacks have been largely absorbed into Black America in general but while they were distinguishable, they showed that American Blacks had the capacity to achieve. For example, in 1950, about 60% of Black professionals in Washington DC had a paternal ancestor who was a free person of color, even though only 12% of the ancestors of Blacks in general were such; and about 80% of American Blacks who received a PhD were descended from free persons. The descendents of free persons of color have a higher proportion of White ancestry than Blacks in general, but there is no evidence that White ancestry has been advantageous within the group (Sowell, 1978b, pp. 8-13, 18, & 25).

West Indian Blacks who come to America constitute, initially at least, a group apart from the larger Black community. They tend to settle in the New York City metropolitan area and their children show a surprising level of achievement. The 1970 census gave the second generation of West Indian Blacks a family income above the national median, equal to the New York City median, and 95% the median of New York City Whites. They had an occupational profile above that of both the nation and New York City, roughly equal to that of New York City Whites. West Indian Blacks are also descended for the most part from 19th century slaves but West Indian slavery differed from the cotton plantation slavery of the American South. Since only 10% of the population were White, Black slaves grew their own food and marketed the surplus, rather than being unskilled field hands who did little but pick cotton. All occupations up to the leisured elite had to be filled by Blacks and Black self-esteem was enhanced. According to Sowell, West Indian immigrants come primarily from nonelite groups and have a higher proportion of African ancestry than native American Blacks, which calls genetic barriers to Black achievement into question (Bureau of the Census, 1972, pp. 4-5 & 570-571; Sowell, 1975, pp. 96-102, 1978b, pp. 41-48, 1978c, p. 258).

In sum, the cotton plantation slavery peculiar to the American South made a difference. Imagine that one of the repeated movements to return plantation slaves to Africa had succeeded in 1850. Then America would have about 13% of its present Black population, about 4 million people, and there would simply be no serious race problem in America today. Blacks would be held up as a marvellous success story proving America's capacity to accommodate all races and creeds. The plausibility of this contention is enhanced by the fact that the descendents of free persons of color saw many of their gains eradicated by the arrival of cotton plantation Blacks, the millions who engulfed them and their neighborhoods during the urban migration that began in 1900. Self-help organizations were overwhelmed, residential and school segregation imposed, Black schools of academic excellence lost their character, prosperous businesses with a White clientele were destroyed (Sowell, 1975, pp. 122-124; 1978b, pp. 35-36).

Cotton plantation Blacks were freed from slavery in 1865 but until World War I, most were bound to the soil by a peonage based on debt and intimidation. Some had acquired skills before emancipation but these eroded as occupations were forbidden them in an opportunity-less rural South. They began the process of urbanization in 1900 and by 1970 almost 80% of Blacks lived in urban centers. The cotton plantation Blacks who flooded into America's cities were more like the Irish than any other of the earlier immigrant groups: both came from a peasantry without self-motivated work or an educational tradition; both had been assigned to the lowest rung of a caste society, the one by slavery, the other by the penal laws which forbade Catholics to purchase land, practice commerce, or enter the professions (Glazer & Moynihan, 1970, p. lxiv; Sowell, 1975, pp. 47-55, & 145-148, 1978b, pp. 29-31; Woodham-Smith, 1962, pp. 27-28).

However, there were important differences. Blacks lacked the Irish political tradition and as late as the 1960s, the Irish-dominated New York police force, with every member, friend and relative voting, may well have exercised more political influence than the entire population of Harlem (Flynn, 1967, pp. 173-174). Blacks were religiously divided and lacked the parochial schools the Catholic Irish had enjoyed.

Moynihan as an Irishman watching Jewish Americans gain ascendancy in New York lamented the mediocrity of Catholic education; but Sowell watching Blacks leave public schools illiterate and innumerate envied the Irish their schools as if they were a priceless asset, where one could get an education in an orderly classroom, under dedicated and sympathetic staff, who believed their pupils were educable. When Sowell isolated Black schools with a history of excellence, three of the five currently effective turned out to be parochial schools. The Irish did not target themselves to universities with the same efficiency as the Chinese, but at least they did not suffer the ravages of "affirmative action". Sowell found that a whole generation of Black college students were the victims of a body count. Universities filled their Black quota by allocating Blacks to various colleges irrespective of educational background and viability. Blacks struggled at great universities who could have passed and profited at average universities, and so on down the line, with the result that often half of all Black students were failures recorded or concealed (Glazer & Moynihan, 1970, p. lxii & 237-238; Sowell, 1972, pp. 130-132, 184-185, & 208-216, 1986, pp. 10-32, 1989).

Nonetheless, in 1970, there were grounds for guarded optimism. A few groups came to America with the advantage of an urban background, or a highly unusual rural background like the Chinese. But for most groups, their economic progress can be measured by how long they have lived in American cities and participated in a modern industrial economy. In 1970, Blacks were relative newcomers: they had become urban residents two or three generations after the Irish with a median year in the 1940s as compared to an Irish median of about 1870. Four-fifths of Blacks in Northern cities were urban immigrants themselves or the children of such and yet, their age-adjusted family income was 79% of the national average. There seemed every reason to believe they would follow the Irish pattern and attain parity over the next two generations, perhaps taking a bit longer because of disadvantages in political influence, schooling, and persistent bias based on appearance (Kessler-Harris & Yans-McLaughlin, 1978, p. 108; Sowell, 1975, pp. 34-35, 49-50, and 152).

Blacks and the Moynihan Report

However, as early as 1965, Daniel Patrick Moynihan saw a cloud on the horizon and in that year, he wrote the famous "Moynihan report". Moynihan had perceived a tendency for Black solo-mother homes to increase independently of certain key economic indicators. He was criticized for saying that a disproportionate number of Black families were "pathological", blaming the Black family for the problems of American Blacks, and going beyond what the evidence would bear. It was argued that the increase in solo-mother homes was small, might not persist, and hardly justified the conclusion that the Black family was in crisis. Moynihan used the language of the day, but since pathological carries unfortunate connotations, I have preferred to discuss whether families are "educationally efficient" or "achievement efficient". The second charge is unjust. Moynihan did not imply that the Black family was some sort of uncaused first cause engendering the environment of Black Americans but unaffected by it; rather he thought of it as a **nexus** of their problems, rather like a key railway junction, where causal lines come together to affect children and thus the next generation. As for the language of crisis, however finely balanced the evidence at the time, subsequent events put the word "crisis" into everyone's mouth from the mass media, to the Urban League, to radical Black sociologists (Jacob, 1984, p. vi; NZPA Staff, 1986, p. 16; Rainwater & Yancey, 1967; Staples, 1985, p. 1005).

The years 1965 to 1990 have seen a trend which has had tragic consequences for at least the lower half of Black America. The percentage of Black men in steady employment has declined and while the percentage fluctuates with the rise and fall of the general level of unemployment, the phenomenon has a life of its own: if one draws a line through the fluctuations, it begins with 75% of Black men in steady work in 1965 and ends with a projection of 50% in 1990. This trend dictates the prospects of Black women and the conditions of Black family life.

Black women do not have more relaxed views about illegitimacy or marriage ties than White women, indeed, they are more likely to want the traditional role of motherhood within the context of a traditional marriage. Their behavior is a compromise between these aspirations and a certain limiting condition: the scarcity of Black males. First, many Black males die young, for example, those born in Harlem are less likely to survive to the age of 40 than children born in Bangladesh. Second, those who do survive are often not promising as permanent partners. Thanks to the scarcity of Black males, Black women must either forgo children, or have them out of wedlock, or have them with husbands whose presence is likely to be temporary. By the close of the 1980s, the grim mathematics that faced Black women ran as follows: for every 100 Black women of marriageable age, there were 95 Black men still alive, the others dead because of differential susceptibility to illness, suicide, murder, or Vietnam; deducting two men in prison left 93 suitable partners; deducting 10 too demoralized to have any fixed residence, and therefore nonlocatable by the census, left 83; deducting 20 located but no longer seeking employment, or at least no longer seeking **lawful** employment, left 63; deducting 12 in intermittent employment left 51, that is, 51 Black males in steady work for every 100 women (Pollard, 1991, p. 8; Staples, 1985, pp. 1006-1009).

As to the effect on Black families, the percentage that are solo-mother is the mirror-image of the number of promising male partners, that is, take the number of Black males in steady work per 100 women, deduct that from 100, and you approximate the percentage of solo-mother homes. In the 1960s, when the number of Black males in steady work stood at 71 per 100 women, solo-mother homes were about 25%; when the number fell to 51 per 100, solo-mother homes rose to 50%. There is nothing intrinsically the matter with a solo-mother home. However, Black solo-mothers tend to be poor, they tend to have more children than other mothers, and the poor among them tend to have more children still. The result is that 63% of Black children being raised in solo-mother homes are below the poverty line. The projection for the 1990s is three-fourths of Black children raised in solo-mother homes and this alone would guarantee 47% of Black children raised in poverty (.63 x 75% = 47%). Differential fertility rates pose a special problem for Blacks not only within each generation but also between generations. The Black middle class underreproduce compared to their White counterparts, while the Black lower class have more offspring than Whites. Thus, going from one generation to the next, fewer Blacks inherit middle class status and a disproportionate number must attempt all over again to win the desperate struggle up out of poverty (Gardner et al., 1985, p. 21; Jacob, 1984, p. vi; NZPA Staff, 1986, p. 16; Sowell, 1975, pp. 135-138; Staples, 1985, pp. 1006, 1009 & 1011; Vaughn-Cooke, 1984, p. 5).

According to Sowell, Black families have never been educationally efficient. Blacks respect education but often do not appreciate the need for persistence, uninterrupted work, and an atmosphere conducive to intellectual interests. The family reinforces achievements with immediate appeal, athletic triumphs, musical promise, more than those that require self-denial or long-range planning.   The child pursuing an intellectual task may not get sufficient psychological support, particularly if the activity interferes with family sociability.   This is a special trait of low-income homes, which underlines the gravity of trends which may put more and more Black children into poverty homes (Sowell, 1972, pp. 228-229; 1975, pp. 130-132).

Willie's study of Black lower class families is bleak, parents who were themselves educational failures and who have lost all hope, who admonish children not to leave school but make no concrete effort at prevention, solo-mothers constantly moving from one job, home, city, and partner to another, their own children beginning motherhood at 16. McGhee's data provide the most depressing fact of all: 36% of Black solo-mother homes report a child suspended or expelled from school for discipline problems. Given what a child must do in an American public school to earn these sanctions, this stands as a sign that a majority of these children are pursuing formal education in name only (McGhee, 1984, p. 240; Willie, 1978, p. 51).

No one has a full explanation of the trend toward fewer Black men in steady work but two factors stand out: the contrast between the labor market today and that faced by groups who arrived in urban centers some generations ago; the growth of the alternative drug economy. Industry requires fewer and fewer unskilled workers and negotiated rates of pay favor the skilled. At one time, low wages made it profitable to hire the less skilled, less experienced, less reliable, and even children could find work; today high wages dictate buying higher skills and labor-saving devices. On the other hand, where the demand for unskilled labor is increasing, for service workers outside industry, low wages create their own problems. The fast food chains give teenagers generous spending money but only those who rise in the hierarchy can afford to support a family. Raising the minimum wage is no solution because a high minimum wage, just like high award wages, simply makes the unskilled unemployable. The 20th century has also seen an irrational escalation of credentialing. Despite the fact that many jobs have been simplified by technology, flying an airplane, driving a truck, calculating change, employers demand diplomas and degrees from prospective employees. Today a firm may require a university degree of its commercial travellers (Sowell, 1972, p. 290; 1975, pp. 154-155).

The drug traffic is like prohibition in that ineffective laws fail to suppress an irrepressible demand, create a huge and lucrative alternative economy, and provide an economic base for criminal activities ranging from robbery to prostitution. But it is unlike prohibition as an avenue of upward mobility. Under prohibition, Irish, Italian, and Jewish Americans sometimes acquired impressive skills plus the means to help their children move into legitimate occupations. Liquor had to be made or imported, bottled, stored, transported in trucks, and sold at wholesale or retail outlets. Selling drugs at least on the street level is almost totally unstructured and decentralized. An individual can reap large profits with little capital investment and after years of activity, develop no skills or habits transferable to the mainstream economy. It does not provide a foundation for a stable or educationally efficient family. It leads nowhere and yet acts as a powerful magnet pulling Blacks out of legitimate occupations. After the Harlem riots, Bayard Rustin got jobs for 120 Black youths: within a few weeks only 12 were still working; the alternative economy simply offered young Blacks far more money for selling drugs or pimping than they could hope to earn from modest employment (Silberman, 1967, p. 440).

There is a real danger that the economic viability of the lower half of the Black community will deteriorate over the next generation. This does not mean "nothing can be done" and while a detailed program should be the product of many minds and a wide range of expertise, I will sketch my own amateur list of proposals without defending them.

A huge construction program to restore America's decaying infrastructure would provide many semiskilled jobs, particularly if the relevant unions are not allowed to bar black labor. A reduction of the minimum wage would create jobs for the unskilled and income supplements could be used selectively, for example: those who were both heads of families and employed would get supplements taking their income up to 120% of the poverty level, making low-paid work compatible with adequate family support; parents with preschool children would receive an income that matched the poverty level; adults who were both without family responsibilities and unemployed would receive 80%, thus leaving incentives to work intact. The fact that Blacks, even when their incomes and educational levels improve, find it harder to move into integrated neighborhoods than other groups would be acknowledged (Gray, 1990). Social forces trap them in inner city areas and schools and therefore, society must upgrade these schools as a collective responsibility. All inner city schools would be upgraded, of course, irrespective of race, but Blacks would benefit disproportionately. Wages and perks of staff would be elevated to whatever level is needed to attract superior, dedicated, and courageous teachers.

The differential fertility problem consists of too few offspring from the Black middle class and too many from the lower class. The middle class themselves will probably solve their half of the problem, as they become second generation, regard their hard-won status as permanent, and risk having more children (Sowell, 1975, pp. 136-137). Lower class women need help to gain greater control over their own fertility: all major food outlets should be required to provide oral contraceptives, free, with advice by a responsible person. The futile attempt to suppress the sale and consumption of hallucinogenic drugs should be replaced by steps to kill the market: the state should legalize a selection of such drugs and provide products as safe as possible at low cost. This would take the profit out of the drug trade and erode the foundations of the alternative economy. The rationality of these proposals, whatever that may be, is not an index of their political and social viability.

THE HISTORY OF THREE GROUPS

Chinese from the Pearl River delta, with its labor-intensive and rice-based agriculture, came to America with a dynamic work ethic which the Irish, habituated by enforced leisure and potato-based agriculture, could not match. Peasant and village China revered education, Confucianism gave dignity to peasant labor and discouraged alcoholism. The Irish used alcohol to enliven lives void of public and private purpose and, partially due to the Penal laws, had an underdeveloped educational tradition. Cotton plantation Blacks came from a slavery and peonage at least as devoid of self-motivated work and educational tradition as the Irish, and arrived at urban centers two or three generations later.

Certain Irish institutions counterproductive vis-à-vis the Chinese take on the character of priceless assets when viewed against the backdrop of the Black experience. The Catholic church with its parochial schools and universities may have given the Irish an education mediocre by comparison with the Chinese, for the latter extracted the best education public schools and great universities had to offer. But Catholic schools gave Irish the literacy and numeracy that led toward the middle class, whereas Blacks faced the worst schools the public system offered. The Irish political machines may have encouraged them to be content with modest civil service jobs and discouraged higher ambitions. If so, the numerical and political weakness of the Chinese removed a temptation and encouraged them to rely on that combination of hard work, sobriety, and maximization of educational capital, which eventually led them to the pinnacle of achievement in American society. On the other hand, political patronage did lift many Irish into the middle class, favoring them over Blacks who became politically dominant only later, their freedom of maneuver limited by entrenched groups and a climate unfavorable to patronage.

Despite these relative disadvantages, as late as 1970, it seemed Blacks could hope to follow the Irish path toward parity. However, the years between 1965 and 1990 saw the development of a trend that threatened to divide Black America into a middle class showing excellent progress in terms of enhanced occupational status, and a lower class whose family structure was becoming less and less educationally efficient. The trend was toward fewer Black males in steady employment. The causes included new conditions in the labor market, thanks to regulation and a shift in the locus of unskilled jobs, and the rise of an alternative economy based on drugs. Other causes as yet unknown are probably operative: the success of the children of free persons of color and West Indian immigrants suggests that these are environmental rather than genetic. Remedies may exist but whether the American political and social system has the flexibility to try them is another question.

8

Epilogue
Setting the Record Straight

The powerful emotions engendered by group differences in test scores, academic achievement, occupation, and income take place in a certain context. That context is the product of human misery. If America can help almost all of its citizens towards a good life, the obsession with total equality between groups will diminish: whether Chinese or Irish or Blacks had exactly the same occupational profile might interest social scientists but not the ordinary person.

Chinese and Japanese Americans focus our attention on the non-IQ factors that cause different ethnic groups to compile different records of achievement. It may be objected that eventually, time will make ethnic groups in America as alike as assimilated subgroups within the White population, thus leaving all groups the captives of their own mean IQs. This objection rests on an unstated assumption: that equalizing the environments of American ethnic groups would leave significant IQ differences intact. That may be false. Asian and White differences would probably disappear with the possible exception of an Asian credit for spatial visualization, but one of no great practical significance. It is quite possible that Black and White differences would also disappear (Flynn, 1980; 1987b; 1989).

As to the nature of the non-IQ factors that affect group achievement, the proximate causes are different IQ thresholds and capitalization rates. I have argued that the ultimate causes are psychological, sociological, and historical, with a clear bias toward an environmental hypothesis. But it is important not to claim more than has been evidenced. The case for potent non-IQ factors is overwhelming, the question of whether these non-IQ factors reflect genetic or environmental differences is still open. Take the fact that Chinese Americans have a more intense work ethnic than Irish Americans, or the fact that they have lower rates of alcoholism. Perhaps there is a genetic component in these group differences and perhaps genes do much to structure the environment. If a group with the relevant Chinese genotypes had settled Ireland, hard work and abstemiousness might have created a dynamic agricultural economy. If a group with Irish genotypes had settled the Pearl River delta, they might have produced a more romantic and Dionysian culture. Rice, potatoes, and cotton may be causes, but not the ultimate level of causality.

Short of an experiment in which Chinese infants are adopted by Irish, without any sense of alienation, and Irish infants adopted by Chinese, these ultimate questions may be difficult to resolve. For the present, I will simply state my reasons for considering environmentalism a promising option. It is quite plausible that genetic differences could give one group on average a higher level of energy than another, but I know of no evidence that Chinese expend a greater sum total of energy than Irish. They differ primarily in what they devote their energy to, work or sport, study or political argumentation. And to say that when two groups have equal energy, one has a genetic proclivity to use it advising a client after normal working hours, the other to use it in a political discussion at a pub, that must be strongly evidenced. Vernon (1982, pp. 188-189) found evidence that Chinese and Japanese share with Native Americans a tendency toward flushing and dizziness from small amounts of alcohol. But note that this genetic proclivity, if it is such, did not prevent alcohol from becoming the bane of Native American peoples, almost the sole exception being the Pueblos whose cultural patterns suppressed it (Benedict, 1946, p. 88).

Genetic differences for character traits may exist between racial groups because of their evolutionary past. However, at present, these theories do little to explain or predict what social scientists want to know. For example, a global hierarchy of the races does not explain why Chinese from the core of the Pearl River delta outperformed those from its periphery, why Protestant Irish achieved parity quickly and Catholic Irish slowly, why some Black groups have approached White income and others remain in poverty. Or to take what may be a fairer example, if one wishes to predict the percentage of illegitimate births and broken marriages among Black women, the percentage of Black males in steady employment is remarkably effective. Positing a genetic proclivity toward early and less disciplined sexual behavior generates no prediction whatsoever about how much or how little Blacks will vary from the White norm.

Before closing: it is not easy to survey the achievements of Chinese and Japanese Americans without emotion. Nothing said herein diminishes their stature, unless someone believes that high achievement is less important than better genes, or that achievement with average IQ is less worthy than achievement with high IQ. Brand (1984, p. 309) did well to celebrate the contributions Chinese and Japanese have made to American life despite hardship and prejudice. But the record must be set straight: they did all of this without an advantage in mean IQ. There is an irony in the fact that they overcame bias wherever they encountered it and yet, never excelled on the putatively unbiased IQ test.

Appendix A
Matarazzo's Data (from p. 69)

Matarazzo (1972, pp. 166 and 177-180) provided scores for enlisted men from various occupations who took the Army General Classification Test (AGCT) during World War II; and IQ scores for medical students, Ph.D. candidates, and university scientists who took the Wechsler Adult Intelligence Scale (WAIS). The occupational categories of Matarazzo and the census were similar but not identical. For elite professions, I matched accountant, college professor, engineer, chemist, lawyer, and physician (IQ data) with accountant, architect, college professor, engineer, natural scientist, lawyer and judge, clergyman, and physician (census). For the less exclusive occupations, I matched artist, teacher, and pharmacist (IQ data) with artist and writer, teacher, nurse, and technician (census).

Using Matarazzo's data as presented, the elite professions would have a mean IQ of 122, all professions plus technicians 115. However, his data must be adjusted. For the AGCT, he gave the conventional values of mean = 100 and SD = 20. The Staff, Personnel Research Section, Adjutant General's Office (1945, pp. 761-764) originally normed the AGCT on a substandard sample and almost immediately began to get groups with inflated means and SDs as high as 23. The norms were adjusted to give reasonable results for draftees, but draftees omitted elite groups such as officers and those with occupational deferments and included all races. The attenuated *SD* was never corrected. To get values based on a truly representative sample, I took Davenport (1946, p. 591), who gave AGCT distributions for various educational categories, and projected his data on the 1940 census, White males aged 20 to 29 years. The results were mean = 101.80 and *SD* = 22.5 (circa 1942). These values reduce the occupational means calculated from AGCT scores by 3 IQ points. As for Matarazzo's WAIS data, allowing for obsolescence reduces the means by 2 or 3 points.

Using the adjusted data, the elite professions have a mean IQ of 119, all professions plus technicians 112. To calculate thresholds, I assumed that each mean was the result of a threshold cutting off the upper portion of the IQ distribution. For example, if the threshold for the elite professions was 110, this would cut off the top 25.25% of a normal curve and the mean IQ of the top 25.25% is 119. The threshold for all professions plus technicians would be 100. These values are not meant to suggest that occupational IQ thresholds provide rigid prerequisites for admission: although nurses or technicians will normally have above average IQs, there will of course be exceptions. Matarazzo's AGCT data suggest that at least 90% score above the theoretical IQ thresholds. It is gratifying that Gottfredson (1987, p. 511) derived thresholds for physician and engineer which, when converted into White norms, are identical with my own.

Appendix B
Key Values for the SAT (from p. 85)

The key value required to convert SAT scores onto a scale analogous to IQ scores is a White population SD expressed in SAT points. The full list of key values needed to estimate the mean IQs of Asian and White candidates who sat the SAT in 1971-1972 is as follows: the percentage of the population cohort the candidate group represents; a correlation coefficient between taking the SAT and IQ; the mean IQ and SD of the population cohort or at least the general population. An example may illustrate how these values would help. Assume the top 27.5% of Whites took the SAT and that the correlation between taking the SAT and IQ was perfect. Then the mean IQ of the candidates would be 1.215 SDs above the population mean, or 18 IQ points above the population mean (1.215 x 15 = 18), or an IQ of 118 (100 + 18 = 118). The correlation is not perfect, of course. But with a correlation of say .60, multiplying that times 18 would give 11 points to be added to the population mean, and would give Whites who sat the SAT a mean IQ of 111. I will derive the SAT key values in the order in which they have been listed.

The first, White population SDs expressed in SAT points, comes from a representative sample of high school seniors who were given the SAT in 1966. They had SDs of 126 for the SAT-M and 120 for the SAT-V. However, these high school seniors were an elite group because at that time, only about 82% of the relevant age cohort reached the 12th grade. Computer projections suggest values for the general population of 139 and 129 respectively. The general population includes all races and for Whites only the *SDs* would be less, something like 130 for the SAT-M and 120 for the SAT-V (Bureau of the Census, 1970, DC:US, Table 197; Educational Testing Service, 1968-1969, p. 23, 1971, p. 19; Flynn, 1984b, p. 31; Retherford & Sewell, 1988, p. 11; Wirtz, 1977, p. 4).

The second key value, the percentage of the population cohort the candidate group represents, poses a problem. The 1971-1972 data give SAT results only for those who took the test as seniors and declared their ethnicity. Subsequent years give more complete results for the candidate group, those who take the test at any time whether as sophomores, juniors, or seniors, and additional data on declaration of ethnicity. The subsequent data suggest that the 502,990 Whites whose scores were reported in 1971-1972 were part of a larger candidate group, a group numbering 890,000 which would be 27.5% of the relevant age cohort. The 10,097 Asians reported were part of a group numbering 15,500 which would be 52% of the relevant age cohort. The Asian estimate makes sense in terms of trends over time, that is, the percentage of Asians taking the SAT has gradually risen from about 50% in 1970, to 61% in 1980, to 67% in 1985. The missing candidates would lower both the White and Asian mean scores on the SAT a bit in that those who sit as juniors are a mild elite. But they should not much affect what concerns us, the difference between the White and Asian means, and indeed, subsequent years show very similar Asian/White differences (Educational Testing Service, 1971-1972 to 1981, 1988, p. v; Gardner, Robey, & Smith, 1985, p. 27; Hsia, 1983, p. 131, 1988, pp. 26 & 63-74; Jackson, 1976, p. 6; Wirtz, 1977, p. 4).

The third key value, a correlation coefficient between taking the SAT and IQ, has been estimated in two steps. The initial step is to calculate the correlation between taking the SAT and performance on the SAT itself. The best method is to compare the scores of the candidate group of 1966-1967 with a nationwide sample of high school seniors tested in 1966 (Educational Testing Service, 1968-1969, p. 23; Jackson, 1976, pp. 6 & 16; Wirtz, 1977, p. 4). The former represented the upper 27.5% or a group 1.215 *SDs* above the population mean; the latter, thanks to the fact that only the upper 82% of the relevant age cohort reached the 12th grade, a group .320 *SDs* above. The difference between the two gives us an ideal score gap, the gap that would exist were the correlation perfect: 1.215 - .320 = .895 *SDs*. The actual score gap between the SAT candidates and all high school seniors was 74.5 SAT-V points or .578 *SDs* (74.5 ÷ 129 as SAT-V population *SD*). Since the correlation coefficient is a measure of the failure to regress to the mean, it can be estimated by dividing the actual score gap by the ideal score gap: .578 *SD* ÷ .895 *SDs* = .65 as SAT-V correlation coefficient. The value for the SAT-M would be .72.

The next step is to use the correlation between taking the SAT and performance on the SAT as a rough guide to the correlation between taking the SAT and performance on IQ tests. I have assumed that whatever academic hurdles prevent or discourage students from taking the SAT, those hurdles have a higher correlation with SAT scores than IQ scores. This seems safe enough in that the SAT has a greater admixture of school learning than most IQ tests. On the other hand, IQ should not lag far behind: the SAT and at least Cattell IQs correlate at the .81 level (Razz et al., 1983), which is as high as IQ tests correlate with one another. Therefore, I decided to put the correlation between taking the SAT-V and verbal IQ at .50, the correlation between taking the SAT-M and nonverbal IQ at .60. By way of apology, a modest deviation from these values has little effect on our overall results.

The final key value, population IQ means and *SDs,* are set at 100 and 15 respectively for Whites. Since the Asians in question are mainly Chinese and Japanese, the *SD* values from the Coleman Report stand, namely, 15.41 for verbal IQ and 18.07 for nonverbal IQ. I have calculated mean IQs for the Asian population as a whole in terms of the ethnic composition of the SAT candidate group. Strictly speaking, the Asian population should be left unaltered, means calculated for each ethnic subpopulation, and these used to calculate means for each subgroup within the candidate group. However, the simpler method allows the calculations to be spelled out and gives, if anything, a slight underestimate of Asian overperformance.

The ethnic composition of the Asian SAT candidate group was determined as described on p. 84, the detailed breakdown being 41% Japanese, 39% Chinese, 10% Filipino, and 10% other, mainly Korean and Asian Indian. The existent data on Filipinos (see Table 7.1) suggest that their mean is about 13 points below Chinese and Japanese. No real data exist for Koreans and Asian Indians but their academic profile is far closer to Chinese than Filipino. Therefore, I calculated mean IQs for the relevant Asian population by taking the values for Chinese and Japanese and simply allowing for the Filipino deficit. The value for verbal IQ drops from 96.70 to 95.38, the value for nonverbal IQ drops from 100.25 to 98.93.

See the bottom of Table 5.3 on p. 86 for the calculations that utilize all of the SAT key values.

References

Anastasi, A. (1968). *Psychological testing* (3rd ed.). New York: Macmillan.

Backman, M.E. (1972). Patterns of mental abilities: Ethnic, socio-economic and sex differences. *American Educational Research Journal, 9*, 1-12.

Basiuk, V. (1984). Security recedes. *Foreign Policy, 53*, 49-73.

Bell, D.A. (1985). The triumph of Asian-Americans. *The New Republic*, July 15 and 22.

Benedict, R. (1946). *Patterns of culture* (Mentor ed.). New York: The New American Library.

Bodde, D. (1957). *China's cultural tradition: What and whither?* New York: Rinehart.

Brand, C.R. (1984). Japanese IQ. *Bulletin of the British Psychological Society, 37*, 308-9.

Brand, D. (1987). The new whiz kids: Why Asian Americans are doing so well, and what it costs them. *Time*, August 31.

Bryan, M.M. (1965). Stanford Achievement Test (1964 revision). In O.K. Buros (Ed.), *The sixth mental measurements yearbook* (pp. 109-124). Highland Park, NJ: The Gryphon Press.

Burch, R.T. (1953). California Arithmetic Test. In O.K. Buros (Ed.), *The fourth mental measurements yearbook* (pp. 511-512). Highland Park, NJ: The Gryphon Press.

Bureau of the Census, 1940, Sixteenth Census of the United States, *Characteristics of the population, 2nd series, Hawaii population*. Washington, DC: Government Printing Office.

Bureau of the Census, 1960, Eighteenth Decennial Census of the United States, *Characteristics of the population, part 13, Hawaii*. Washington, DC: Government Printing Office.

Bureau of the Census, 1960 Census of the Population, PC(2)-1C, *Nonwhite population by race* . Washington, DC: Government Printing Office.

Bureau of the Census, 1970 Census of the Population, *Detailed characteristics: United States summary*. Washington, DC: Government Printing Office.

Bureau of the Census, 1970 Census of the Population, PC(2)-1G, *Japanese, Chinese, and Filipinos in the United States*. Washington, DC: Government Printing Office.

Bureau of the Census, 1972, *County and City Data Book*. Washington, DC: Government Printing Office.

Bureau of the Census, 1980 Census of the Population, PC80-1-C1, *General social and economic characteristics*. Washington, DC: Government Printing Office.

Bureau of the Census, 1980 Census of the Population, PC80-1-D1-A, *Detailed population characteristics*. Washington, DC: Government Printing Office.

Butterfield, F. (1990). Why they excel. *Parade*, January 21.

Chan, J. (1976). Is Raven's Progressive Matrices Test culture-free or culture-fair? In *Proceedings of the Third IACCP Congress*. Tilbury, England.

Coleman, J.S. et al. (1966a). *Equality of educational opportunity*. Washington, DC: U.S. Office of Education.

Coleman, J.S. et al. (1966b). *Equality of educational opportunity, supplemental appendix, section 9.10, correlation tables*. Washington, DC: U.S. Office of Education.

Davenport, R.K. (1946). Implications of military selection and classification in relation to Universal Military Training. *Journal of Negro Education, 15*, 585-594.

de Lemos, M. (1989). Effects of relative age within grade: Implications for the use of age-based norms for group tests of general ability. *Bulletin of the International Test Commission, 28-29*, 21-44.

Doerner, W.R. (1985). Asians: To America with skills. *Time*, July 8.

Easley, H. (1941). Henmon-Nelson Test of Mental Ability. In O.K. Buros (Ed.), *The nineteen-forty mental measurements yearbook* (p. 222). Highland Park, NJ: The Mental Measurements Yearbook.

East-West Center, Population Institute, *Resource materials collection, special unpublished tabulations of the Asian American population (1980 census)*. Available from Robert Gardner, East-West Center, Honolulu, Hawaii.

Educational Testing Service (1955). *Cooperative School and College Ability Tests, examiner's manual*. Princeton, NJ: ETS Cooperative Test Division.

Educational Testing Service (1957). *Cooperative School and College Ability Tests, technical report*. Princeton, NJ: ETS Cooperative Test Division.

Educational Testing Service (1961). *Cooperative School and College Ability Tests, handbook, level U*. Princeton, NJ: ETS Cooperative Test Division.

Educational Testing Service (1962). *SCAT-STEP supplement*. Princeton, NJ: ETS Cooperative Test Division.

Educational Testing Service (1968-1969). *College board score reports, 1968-69*. Princeton, NJ: College Entrance Examination Board.

Educational Testing Service (1971). *College board score reports, 1971*. Princeton, NJ: College Entrance Examination Board.

Educational Testing Service (1971-72 to 1981 inclusive). *College bound seniors.* Princeton, NJ: College Entrance Examination Board.

Educational Testing Service (1985). *College bound seniors.* Princeton, NJ: College Entrance Examination Board.

Educational Testing Service (1988). *College bound seniors.* Princeton, NJ: College Entrance Examination Board.

Fairbank, J.K., Reischaur, E.V., & Craig, A.M. (1965). *East Asia: The Modern Transformation.* Boston: Houghton Mifflin.

Feldman, D.H. (1971). Map understanding as a possible crystallizer of cognitive structures. *American Educational Research Journal, 8,* 485-501.

Findley, W.G. (1953). California Achievement Tests. In O.K. Buros (Ed.), *The fourth mental measurements yearbook* (pp. 2-6). Highland Park, NJ: The Gryphon Press.

Flanagan, J.C., & Cooley, W.W. (1966). *Project Talent: One-year follow-up studies.* Pittsburgh: University of Pittsburgh; available from W.W. Cooley.

Flanagan, J.C., Dailey, J.T., Shaycroft, M.F., Gorham, W.A., Orr, D.B., & Goldberg, I. (1962). *Design for a study of American youth.* Boston: Houghton Mifflin.

Flaughter, R.L. (1971). *Project Access research report no. 2: Patterns of test performance by high school students of four ethnic identities.* Princeton, NJ: Educational Testing Service.

Flynn, J.R. (1967). *American politics: a radical view.* Auckland: Blackwood & Janet Paul.

Flynn, J.R. (1980). *Race, IQ and Jensen.* London: Routledge & Kegan Paul.

Flynn, J.R. (1983). Now the great augmentation of the American IQ. *Nature, 301,* 655.

Flynn, J.R. (1984a). IQ gains and the Binet decrements. *Journal of Educational Measurement, 21,* 283-290.

Flynn, J.R. (1984b). The mean IQ of Americans: Massive gains 1932 to 1978. *Psychological Bulletin, 95,* 29-51.

Flynn, J.R. (1985). Wechsler intelligence tests: do we really have a criterion of mental retardation? *American Journal of Mental Deficiency, 90,* 236-244.

Flynn, J.R. (1987a). Massive IQ gains in 14 nations: What IQ tests really measure. *Psychological Bulletin, 101,* 171-191.

Flynn, J.R. (1987b). Race and IQ: Jensen's case refuted. In S. Modgil & C. Modgil (Eds.), *Arthur Jensen: Consensus and controversy* (pp. 221-232). Lewes, England: Falmer Press.

Flynn, J.R. (1987c). The rise and fall of Japanese IQ. *Bulletin of the British Psychological Society, 40,* 459-464.

Flynn, J.R. (1989). Rushton, evolution, and race: An essay on intelligence and virtue. *The Psychologist, 1,* 363-366.

Fowler, H.M. (1953). The Henmon-Nelson Tests of Mental Ability: The Clapp-Young Self-Marking Tests. In O.K. Buros (Ed.), *The fourth mental measurements yearbook* (pp. 398-401). Highland Park, NJ: The Gryphon Press.

Fox, L.H. (1976). Sex differences in mathematical precocity: Bridging the gap. In D.P. Keating (Ed.), *Intellectual talent: Research and development* (pp. 183-214). Baltimore: Johns Hopkins Press.

Gardner, R.W., Robey, B., & Smith, P.C. (1985). *Asian Americans: Growth, change, and diversity.* Washington, DC: Population Reference Bureau.

Glazer, N., & Moynihan, D.P. (1970). *Beyond the melting pot* (2nd ed.). Cambridge, MA: MIT Press.

Gottfredson, L.S. (1987). The practical significance of black-white differences in intelligence. *Behavioral and Brain Sciences, 10,* 510-512.

Gray, H.H. (1990, March). *President of the University - to alumni and other friends.* Chicago: University of Chicago, Office of the President.

Greenwald, J. (1985). Finding niches in a new land. *Time,* July 8.

Grodzins, M. (1949). *Americans betrayed.* Chicago: University of Chicago Press.

Hieronymus, A.N., & Stroud, J.B. (1969). Comparability of IQ scores on five widely used intelligence tests. *Measurement and Evaluation in Guidance, 2,* 135-140.

Hovland, C.I. (1949). Terman-McNemar Test of Mental Ability. In O.K. Buros (Ed.), *The third mental measurements yearbook* (pp. 342-343). Highland Park, NJ: The Gryphon Press.

Hsia, J. (1983). Cognitive assessment of Asian-Americans. In M. Chu-Chang & V. Rodriguez (Eds.), *Asian- and Pacific-American perspectives in bilingual education* (pp. 123-152). New York: Teachers College, Columbia University.

Hsia, J. (1988). *Asian Americans in higher education and at work.* Hillsdale, NJ: Lawrence Erlbaum & Associates.

Hu, C-T. (1962). *Chinese education under Communism.* New York: Teachers College, Columbia University.

Jackson, R. (1976). *A summary of SAT score statistics for college board candidates.* Princeton, NJ: College Entrance Examination Board.

Jacob, J.E. (1984). An overview of Black America in 1983. In J.D. Williams (Ed.), *The state of Black America 1984* (pp. i-vii). New York: National Urban League.

Jencks, C. (1972). *Inequality: A reassessment of the effect of family and schooling in America.* New York: Basic Books.

Jensen, A.R. (circa 1970). *A comparative study of the scholastic achievements of minority and majority pupils in the Bakersfield public schools.* Unpublished manuscript, available from A.R. Jensen, Institute of Human Learning, University of California, Berkeley.

Jensen, A.R. (1973). *Educational differences.* London: Methuen.

Jensen, A.R. (1980). *Bias in mental testing.* London: Methuen.

Jensen, A.R. (1986). Academic work and educational excellence: Raising student productivity. *Educational Evaluation and Policy Analysis, 8,* 447-451.

Jensen, A.R., & Reynolds, C.R. (1982). Race, social class and ability patterns on the WISC-R. *Personality and Individual Differences, 3,* 423-438.

Kanengiser, A. (1985). Asian refugee kids in USA "love to learn." *USA Today,* July 18.

Kaufman, A.S., McLean, J.E., Ishikuma, T., & Moon, S-B. (1986). *Integration of the literature on the intelligence of Japanese children and analysis of the data from a sequential-simultaneous model.* Unpublished manuscript.

Kessler-Harris, A., & Yans-McLaughlin, V. (1978). European immigrant groups. In T. Sowell (Ed.), *Essays and data on American ethnic groups* (pp. 107-137). Washington, DC: The Urban Institute.

Lee, R.H. (1960). *The Chinese in the United States of America.* Hong Kong: University Press.

Lesser, G.S., Fifer, G., & Clark, D.H. (1965). Mental abilities of children from different social-class and cultural groups. *Monographs of the Society for Research in Child Development, 30*, serial no. 102.

Lindsey, R. (1982). The new Asian immigrants. *The New York Times Magazine*, May 9.

Longstreth, L.E. (1978). Level I - Level II abilities as they affect performance of three races in the college classroom. *Journal of Educational Psychology, 70*, 289-297.

Lorge, I., & Thorndike, R.L. (1954). *The Lorge-Thorndike Intelligence Tests, general manual.* Boston: Houghton Mifflin.

Lorge, I., & Thorndike, R.L. (1957). *The Lorge-Thorndike Intelligence Tests, technical manual.* Boston: Houghton Mifflin.

Luh, C.W., & Wu, T.M. (1931). A comparative study of the intelligence of Chinese children on the Pinter performance and the Binet tests. *Journal of Social Psychology, 2*, 402-408.

Lynn, R. (1977). The Intelligence of the Japanese. *Bulletin of the British Psychological Society, 30*, 69-72.

Lynn, R. (1982). IQ in Japan and the United States shows a growing disparity. *Nature, 297*, 222-223.

Lynn, R. (1987a). Japan: Land of the rising IQ. A reply to Flynn. *Bulletin of the British Psychological Society, 40*, 464-468.

Lynn, R. (1987b). The intelligence of the Mongoloids: A psychometric, evolutionary and neurological theory. *Personality and Individual Differences, 8*, 813-844.

Lynn, R., & Hampson, S. (1986). The structure of Japanese abilities: An analysis in terms of the hierarchical model of intelligence. *Current Psychological Research and Reviews, 41*, 309-322.

Lynn, R., Hampson, S., & Lee, M. (1988). The intelligence of Chinese children in Hong Kong. *Social Psychology International, 9*, 29-32.

Lynn, R. (in press). Racial differences in intelligence: A global perspective. *Mankind Quarterly*.

Maccoby, E.E., & Jacklin, C.N. (1973). Sex differences in intellectual functioning. In *Assessment in a pluralist society* (pp. 37-55). Proceedings of the 1972 Invitational Conference on Testing Problems. Princeton, NJ: Educational Testing Service.

Majoribanks, K. (1972). Ethnic and environmental influences on mental abilities. *American Journal of Sociology, 78*, 323-337.

Marsella, A.J., & Golden, C.J. (1980). The structure of cognitive abilities in Americans of Japanese and of European ancestry in Hawaii. *The Journal of Social Psychology, 112*, 19-30.

Matarazzo, J.D. (1972). *Wechsler's measurement and appraisal of adult intelligence* (5th ed.). Baltimore: Williams & Wilkins.

Mayeske, G.W., Okada, T., Cohen, W.M., Beaton, A.E. Jr., & Wisler, C.E. (1973). *A study of achievement of our nation's students.* Washington, DC: U.S. Office of Education.

McAleavy, H. (1967). *The modern history of China.* London: Weidenfeld & Nicolson.

McBee, S. (1984). Asian-Americans: Are they making the grade? *U.S. News and World Report,* April 2.

McDonald, G. (1989). *The normal curve of intelligence: Is this a representation of promotional patterns?* Paper presented at the 11th New Zealand Association for Research into Education (NZARE) Conference, Central Institute of Technology at Heretaunga, Wellington, New Zealand.

McGhee, J.D. (1984). A profile of the Black single female-headed household. In J.D. Williams (Ed.), *The state of Black America 1984* (pp. 43-67).

Menzel, J.M. (1963). Introduction. In J.M. Menzel (Ed.), *The Chinese civil service: Career open to talent?* (pp. vii-xii). Lexington, MA: Heath.

Mittman, A. (1965). Sequential Tests of Educational Progress: Mathematics. In O.K. Buros (Ed.), *The sixth mental measurements yearbook* (pp. 879-881). Highland Park, NJ: The Gryphon Press.

Nagoshi, C.T., & Johnson, R.C. (1987). Cognitive ability profiles of Caucasian vs. Japanese subjects in the Hawaii Family Study of Cognition. *Personality and Individual Differences, 8*, 581-583.

Nichols, R.C. (1987). Racial differences in intelligence. In S. Modgil & C. Modgil (Eds.), *Arthur Jensen: Consensus and controversy* (pp. 213-220). Lewes, England: Falmer Press.

North, R.D. (1959). California Arithmetic Test, 1957 edition. In O.K. Buros (Ed.), *The fifth mental measurements yearbook* (pp. 592-593). Highland Park, NJ: The Gryphon Press.

NZPA Staff (1986). Spotlight on disadvantaged Blacks. *Otago Daily Times,* February 18.

Ohio State University Psychological Test, Form 21, 1941 (1949). In O.K. Buros (Ed.), *The third mental measurements yearbook* (p. 323). Highland Park, NJ: The Gryphon Press.

Petersen, W. (1971). *Japanese Americans: Oppression and success.* New York: Random House.

Petersen, W. (1978). Chinese Americans and Japanese Americans. In T. Sowell (Ed.), *Essays and data on American ethnic groups* (pp. 65-106). Washington, DC: The Urban Institute.

Pinter, R. (1938). Ohio State University Psychological Test. In O.K. Buros (Ed.), *The nineteen thirty-eight mental measurements yearbook* (p. 105). New Brunswick, NJ: Rutgers University Press.

Pollard, S. (1991). Segregated education again to help Black males in US. *Otago Daily Times,* March 1.

Portenier, L.G. (1947). Abilities and interests of Japanese-American high school seniors. *Journal of Social Psychology, 25,* 53-61.

Porteus, S.D., & Babcock, H. (1926). *Temperament and race.* Boston: Badger.

Rainwater, L., & Yancey, W.L. (1967). *The Moynihan report and the politics of controversy.* Cambridge, MA: MIT Press.

Raven, J. (1986). *Manual for Raven's Progressive Matrices and Vocabulary Scales: Research supplement no. 3.* London: H.K. Lewis.

Raven, J., & Court, J.H. (1989). *Manual for Raven's Progressive Matrices and Vocabulary Scales: Research supplement no. 4.* London: H.K. Lewis.

Razz, N., Willerman, L., Ingmundsen, P., & Hanlon, M. (1983). Aptitude-related differences in auditory recognition masking. *Intelligence, 7,* 71-90.

Retherford, R.D., & Sewell, W.H. (1988). *Intelligence and family size reconsidered.* Honolulu: East-West Center.

Rock, D.A., Ekstrom, R.B., Goetz, M.E., Hilton, T.L., & Pollack, J. (1985). *Contractor report: Factors associated with decline of test scores of high school seniors, 1972 to 1980; a study of excellence in high school education, educational policies, school quality, and school outcomes.* Princeton, NJ: Educational Testing Service.

Rushton, J.P. (1989). *Evolutionary biology and heritable traits: With reference to Oriental-White-Black differences.* Paper presented at the Annual Meeting of the American Association for the Advancement of Science, San Francisco, USA.

Rushton, J.P. (1990). *On Rushton, race and academic freedom: Responses from the international academic community* (Report). Unpublished manuscript, available from author.

Schallberger, U. (1985). *HAWIK und HAWIK-R: Ein Empirischer Vergleich* [HAWIK and HAWIK-R: An empirical comparison] (Technical Report). Zurich: Psychologisches Institut der Universität.

Schindler, A.W. (1953). California Achievement Tests. In O.K. Buros (Ed.), *The fourth mental measurements yearbook* (pp. 6-7). Highland Park, NJ: The Gryphon Press.

Schubert, M.T., & Berlach, G. (1982). Neue Richtlinien zur Interpretation des Hamburg Wechsler-Intelligenztests für Kinder (HAWIK) [New guidelines for the interpretation of the Hamburg Wechsler Intelligence Tests for Children (HAWIK)]. *Zeitschrift für Klinische Psychologie, 11,* 253-279.

Silberman, C.E. (1967). Beware the day they change their minds. In L. Rainwater & W.L. Yancy (Eds.), *The Moynihan report and the politics of controversy* (pp. 427-442). Cambridge, MA: MIT Press.

Smith, S. (1942). Language and non-verbal test performance of racial groups in Honolulu before and after a fourteen-year interval. *Journal of General Psychology, 26,* 51-93.

Snyderman, M., & Rothman, S. (1988). *The IQ controversy: The media and public policy*. Brunswick, NJ: Transaction Books.

Sowell, T. (1972). *Black education: myths and tragedies*. New York: David McKay.

Sowell, T. (1975). *Race and economics*. New York: Longman.

Sowell, T. (1978a). Race and IQ reconsidered. In T. Sowell (Ed.), *Essays and data on American ethnic groups* (pp. 203-238). Washington, DC: The Urban Institute.

Sowell, T. (1978b). Three black histories. In T. Sowell (Ed.), *Essays and data on American ethnic groups* (pp. 7-64). Washington, DC: The Urban Institute.

Sowell, T. (1978c). Statistical data on American ethnic groups. In T. Sowell (Ed.), *Essays and data on American ethnic groups* (pp. 253-415). Washington, DC: The Urban Institute.

Sowell, T. (1986). *Education: Assumptions versus history*. Stanford, CA: Hoover Institution Press.

Sowell, T. (1989, December): "Affirmative action": A worldwide disaster. *Commentary*, 21-41.

Sowell, T., & King, H.B. (1975). *Ethnic minorities IQ data file*. National Technical Information Service, Springfield, VA, 22161 (Accession number PB 265 8.13).

Stake, R.E., & Hastings, J.T. (1965). Stanford Achievement Test (1964 revision). In O.K. Buros (Ed.), *The sixth mental measurements yearbook* (pp. 124-128). Highland Park, NJ: The Gryphon Press.

Staples, R. (1985). Changes in Black family structure: The conflict between family ideology and structural conditions. *Journal of Marriage and the Family, 47*, 1005-1013.

Stevenson, H.W., Azuma, H., & Hakuta, K. (1986). *Child development and education in Japan*. New York: Freeman.

Stevenson, H.W., Stigler, J.W., Lee, S., Lucker, G.W., Kitamura, S., & Hsu, C. (1985). Cognitive performance and academic achievement of Japanese, Chinese, and American children. *Child Development, 56*, 718-734.

Stewart, L.H., Dole, A.A., & Harris, Y.Y. (1967). Cultural differences in abilities during high school. *American Educational Research Journal, 4*, 19-30.

Sue, D.A., & Kirk, B.A. (1972). Psychological characteristics of Chinese-American students. *Journal of Counseling Psychology, 19*, 471-478.

Sue, D.W., & Kirk, B.A. (1973). Differential characteristics of Japanese-American and Chinese-American college students. *Journal of Counseling Psychology, 20*, 142-148.

Tan, T.T. (1986). *Your Chinese roots: The overseas Chinese story*. Singapore: Times Book International.

The Staff, Personnel Research Section, Adjutant General's Office (1945). The Army General Classification Test. *Psychological Bulletin, 42*, 760-768.

Thurstone, L.L., & Thurstone, G.T. (1954a). *SRA Primary Mental Abilities, examiner manual, ages 7 to 11* (2nd ed.). Chicago: Science Research Associates.

Thurstone, L.L., & Thurstone, G.T. (1954b). *SRA Primary Mental Abilities, technical supplement, ages 7 to 11* (1st ed.). Chicago: Science Research Associates.

Tiegs, E.N., & Clark, W.W. (1963). *California Achievement Tests complete battery, advanced forms W, X, Y* (1957 ed.). Del Monte Research Park, Monterey, CA: California Test Bureau.

Tuddenham, R.D. (1969). A "Piagetian" test of cognitive development. In W.B. Dockrell (Ed.), *On intelligence: the Toronto symposium on intelligence, 1969* (pp. 49-70). London: Methuen.

Vaughn-Cooke, D. (1984). The economic state of Black America - is there a recovery? In J.D. Williams (Ed.), *The state of Black America 1984* (pp. 1-23). New York: National Urban League.

Vernon, P.E. (1982). *The abilities and achievements of Orientals in North America.* New York: Academic Press.

Wang, S.L. (1926). A demonstration of the language difficulty involved in comparing racial groups by means of verbal intelligence tests. *Journal of Applied Psychology, 10,* 102-106.

Wang, Y.C. (1966). *Chinese intellectuals and the West, 1872-1949.* Chapel Hill, NC: University of North Carolina Press.

Werner, E.E., Simonian, K., & Smith, R.S. (1968). Ethnic and socioeconomic status differences in abilities and achievement among preschool and school-age children in Hawaii. *The Journal of Social Psychology, 75,* 43-59.

Weyl, N. (1966). *The creative elite in America.* Washington, DC: Public Affairs Press.

Weyl, N. (1969). Some comparative performance indexes of American ethnic minorities. *Mankind Quarterly, 9,* 106-119.

Willie, C.V. (1978). The Black family and social class. In R. Staples (Ed.), *The Black family: Essays and studies* (2nd ed., pp. 236-243). Belmont, CA: Wadsworth.

Wing, H. (1980). Profiles of cognitive ability of different racial/ethnic and sex groups on a multiple abilities test battery. *Journal of Applied Psychology, 65,* 289-298.

Wirtz, W. (Chairperson). (1977). *On further examination: Report of the Advisory Panel on the Scholastic Aptitude Test Score Decline.* Princeton, NJ: College Entrance Examination Board.

Woodham-Smith, C. (1962). *The great hunger.* London: Hamish Hamilton.

Yee, L.Y., & La Forge, R. (1974). Relationship between mental abilities, social class, and exposure to English in Chinese fourth graders. *Journal of Educational Psychology, 66,* 826-834.

Author Index

Note: Unless cited as authors, persons mentioned are listed in the Subject Index, for example, Archimedes, Cromwell, and so forth.

Subject Index

Note: Unless of independent interest, subjects are listed under broader headings. Examples: various IQ studies under the ethnic group tested; various IQ tests under the heading "IQ tests".